Fighting FOR MY LIFE

How I Found God and Beat Lyme Disease

PATRICK COLLINS

ISBN: 978-1-4834-6659-0 (sc)
ISBN: 978-1-4834-6660-6 (e)

Library of Congress Control Number: 2017903472

Lulu Publishing Services rev. date: 03/16/2017

Contents

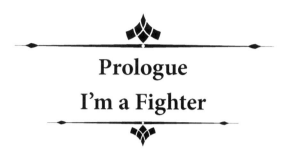

Prologue
I'm a Fighter

As I made the final turn, I could see the finish line, yet it seemed so far away. I saw the clock ticking upward ever so slowly; I saw my coach at the finish line and hundreds of people along barricades cheering for me. I could see everything I had worked so hard for, but I had to run, to make it. I felt every muscle in my body tighten—pain in my legs, pain in my lungs.

But this was nothing compared to the physical, emotional, and psychological pain of the past three years of my life. All the days I couldn't walk because my joints hurt so badly; all the days I wished I were dead.

As I ran, I thought about every day my dad had to wrestle me out of bed to force me to go to school. I thought about the days I wouldn't wake up at all and slept twenty-six hours straight. I thought about the fire of emotions I felt: contempt, agony, rage, depression, disdain, frustration, and apathy. All the suffering ignited by one tick.

I felt I had no energy left, but I broke out into a dead sprint for the finish. I crossed the finish line shattering my previous personal best time. I pounded my chest twice and pointed to the sky, knowing in that moment that there was a God—a God who I'd fallen away from so completely while I was ill, a God who had been with me my entire journey, a God who was forming me into the person He wanted me to become.

Long before that race, long before I took my first steps, said my first words, or even set foot in this world, I was deemed a fighter. I was a twin in the womb, but almost seven months into the pregnancy, my twin died because of a blood clot in the umbilical cord. Because my mother had already had two pregnancies and two miscarriages, the doctors insisted on an emergency C-section.

On January 10, 1997, I entered this world, a two-pound, ten-ounce preemie. My mother says that I wrapped my whole hand around her pinky a few minutes after I was born, and that was her sign from God that I would be okay.

I was put on life support, and my mother couldn't see me for two days. The doctors categorized me as failure to thrive, meaning I was a gaunt newborn only seven inches long and wasn't gaining any weight.

For several weeks in the hospital, my longevity was doubtful at best. I was the child without a name, the other baby. I assume my parents neglected to name me then as a means of preventing their devastation if I passed. It could be a nameless grave. But I was more than the other baby; I was the one who had survived. However, everyone always just called me the Fighter.

After several weeks, my parents had hope of my survival, and as I became more stable, I was given the name Patrick after my great-grandfather Patrick Doran, my mother's grandfather. My grandmother (my mom's mom) surprised them when they arrived home with a pot roast that weighed four pounds. To this day, my grandmother teases my mom and me that the roast she made was bigger than the baby my mom brought home.

I was unable to speak or walk until I was three, but I was the lucky one, the one who had beaten the odds. I have no remaining sadness from that time of my life because I realize that it could have been worse.

I vaguely remember times in preschool that I had unsure footing and often stumbled around the classroom. I realized that this physical instability wouldn't hold me back. I have learned to never listen to those who doubt me because they are toxic. I was born with a purpose. Any goal, aspiration, or ambition I may pursue can easily be crushed by self-doubt with just a few negative words from those who don't believe in me. But I'm the Fighter.

In many ways, I began the typical American childhood in a loving family. I am the youngest of three. My sister Alicia is four years my senior, but she has always been my best friend, and our relationship has always gone much deeper than your average brother-sister relationship. She's the one I look up to and admire. My other sister, Mikaela, has always been either my best friend or my worst enemy. Even as young children, we created devious plans to torture our babysitters or trick our parents. One day, when she was ten and I was eight, Mikaela and I were feeling especially defiant. It was raining, and we were told by our longtime babysitter, Meghan, that we were not to go outside. While Meghan was in the bathroom, Mikaela stood outside the bathroom and yelled, "Patrick, let's go outside!"

"Yeah, let's go now!" I said.

We ran downstairs. Mikaela opened the back door and slammed it shut. We went to different parts of the house to hide. Alicia was in on the scheme. She told Meghan, "You check outside and I'll check inside."

Meghan went outside into the pouring rain to search for us. Alicia called us out of hiding, and we locked all the doors. We let her back in after about an hour.

Though Mikaela and I took great joy in constructing elaborate plans such as that one, on the other side of the spectrum, we often butted heads. She was more interested in school while my interest was sports; she was the nerd and I was the jock. That led to much teasing and name-calling between us but never any physical altercations.

Despite our devilish actions, my family was devotedly Catholic; we went to church every Sunday. We lived in Attleboro, a small city in Massachusetts. My father was a cantor at our church, and my mom was a consultant for the United States Postal Service and was almost always traveling, so I usually found myself with my sisters during services as my father's voice echoed through the building. My family prayed before every meal, giving thanks for the food we ate and the house we lived in. The ideology drilled into me was that all problems could be solved by prayer. And usually, that was applicable to my childhood problems.

Even as I grew past infancy, my health was always an issue. I began kindergarten weighing twenty pounds. Having been born weighing two pounds, I never caught up in weight. Every time I got a cold or the flu, it was a life-threating issue due to my medical history. I was so small that my mom had to have my uniforms custom made for the Catholic school I attended.

Several years later, she told me that before my first day of kindergarten when she picked my uniforms up, the tailor had said, "How cute! You're making doll clothes." My mom was ashamed and grew increasingly resentful about sending me to school.

To help me gain weight, my doctor put me on a high-calorie shake regimen. Those shakes were almost like steroids. Between kindergarten and first grade, my weight doubled from twenty to forty pounds; it had doubled again by the start of second grade to eighty pounds. I eventually surpassed my classmates in physical stature, but I still had a significant achievement gap. Due to my prematurity, I didn't learn to read and write proficiently until the end of second grade. Throughout elementary school, I found writing, concentrating, and sitting still to be extremely difficult because of this.

After a short period of being the smallest of my classmates, I developed a scrappy nature. I was short tempered and easily angered. Suspecting more than just my cognitive issues were contributing to my academic deficit, my parents had me tested and found I had attention deficit hyperactivity disorder (ADHD), which premature babies are twice as likely to develop as are full-term babies.[1] However, that was nothing compared to the impairments I could have faced.

Always being small, I felt I was constantly being picked on. I started many fights with my sisters as well as with my classmates because I didn't have great control over my anger. To avoid pumping me full of stimulants as well as to provide an outlet for my temper, my parents signed me up for football. After the first year of playing, football seemed to be a positive outlet for my aggression. While I was in season, I could better manage my temper, and my hyperactivity was mitigated.

During the last game of my second year of football, I suffered a severe concussion. A malicious hit from behind left me unconscious and disoriented during the third quarter of a playoff game. I was unconscious for about ten seconds. I got up slowly, but no one knew anything was wrong. I finished the game but received countless postconcussive hits. By the end, I was in a state of addled incoherency and was vomiting uncontrollably. I was rushed to the hospital. I missed two months of school due to the injury. The concussion further exacerbated my cognitive difficulties for a time.

I was drowning in a sea of confusion and headaches. I needed a fresh start. I could no longer keep up in the classroom after having missed two months. Instead of spending every day struggling, in fourth grade, my parents and I agreed it would be best for me to transfer from my school in Attleboro to St. Stephan's Academy, a private school in Johnston, Rhode Island. After shadowing for a day and officially transferring on the fourteenth of February, Cupid's arrow struck me; I fell in love with the school.

St. Stephan's seemed like a bit of an overachiever's school. The school from which I transferred paled in comparison to St. Stephan's with its massive, multimillion-dollar building. It had the biggest and the best of everything—that's what I loved about it.

During my first year, I made many new friends, some of whom I consider the best friends I have ever had. I could no longer play football, so I played baseball and basketball. I led my fifth-grade basketball team to a state championship and led the team in scoring. The smaller class size at St. Stephan's also fostered my creativity while corralling my hyperactivity.

In sixth grade, I had my first girlfriend—well, the sixth-grade version of a girlfriend. She had brown hair and blue eyes that made me wonder if I had fallen in love for the first time. I was playing Sonny in the school musical *Grease*. My schedule that winter was entirely booked with schoolwork as well as play and baseball practices. I was a proud member of the Attleboro Badgers baseball team, and I looked forward to a spring filled with practices and games with my friends.

That time was blissful; I had everything I could have asked for—a loving family, a great school, good grades, great friends, and my entire life ahead of me. I was starting to grow in my ideas about what life meant.

My increased respect for life was induced by the death of my uncle Brad. I had never met my dad's brother, but I knew it wasn't right for anyone to suffer as much as he had during his six-month battle with cancer of the appendix. Even when he was in hospice care, he didn't give up. When my dad came back from seeing him, he promised me he'd bring me on the next trip to see him. Unfortunately, that trip never came.

About a month before he passed, we were sure my uncle would die soon. I began to pray the rosary—as I had been taught in religion class—every night. I prayed for that entire month, but after thousands of Hail Marys and Our Fathers, my uncle still passed away. I began to question the existence of God because my prayers hadn't been answered. My father assured me that my prayers had been heard but that God just needed another angel. That confused me. Was anyone listening?

After Uncle Brad died, my family and I went to clean out his apartment. It was an eerie feeling being where he used to live. The creaks I heard in the apartment made me think someone was still there, but I wasn't afraid. That was the first time I had felt the presence of another force. Whether it was God or a spirit I'll never know, but something was definitely there with me that gave me closure and told me my uncle was at peace. The other force felt like a warm embrace reminding me that everything would be okay. I knew Uncle Brad was in a better place wherever that was. My faith told me he was in heaven with God, but my gut told me he was all around me.

What I had been taught in Catholic school was that this world is only temporary as we prepare for eternal life with God as Jesus did. My uncle had suffered tremendously—more than I thought humanly possible—so when he passed, my family should have been thankful he was no longer suffering, but losing him was still devastating. My family and I kept the faith and believed that God had a bigger plan in action. People often say, "Everything happens for a reason," but that implies God intends suffering. I was certain God hadn't given my uncle cancer. I knew God was with my family and my uncle through the entire process.

After that experience, I made it a point to never make anyone or anything suffer as much as he did. I made a vow to never kill anything. I decided to become a vegetarian. I think this was my first real connection with God though I didn't know it.

As sixth grade continued, I tried new things and began to discover who I was—a diligent student, a dedicated athlete, a whimsical classmate, a great friend, and apparently a respectable actor. I was determined to keep dreaming and never let anything stop me. Whenever I was ambivalent about school, my parents reminded me of my past. They reminded me of all I had overcome and that I had a purpose. When they said, "We love you," I knew they meant it. I trusted them.

I felt like an average twelve-year-old in an average town and in an average-income household in an average, structured family. Even my name, Patrick Collins, was average. Something much worse than typical was about to happen, though, something that would test every bit of my resolve and my faith.

Chapter 1
Not Listening

At first, I was upset that our school required a weeklong retreat—a nature adventure—at Camp Crescent Moon in southern Rhode Island. I wasn't happy because I knew I would have to miss a week of baseball, but the retreat also meant spending a week with my best friends.

About a month before we went on the trip, representatives from the camp came to our school and gave us a presentation on what to expect during our time there. We were told that the campgrounds consisted of hundreds of acres of nature reserves, animals from livestock to donkeys, wire fences, bales of hay, and miles of open fields. The greenhouses were used to grow organic food. There was no technology or any sign of modern life. The trip was intended to educate us about how to live without relying on computers. Self-reliance was what we were expected to learn. Though I felt I'd be out of my element, I thought about all the time I would be able to spend with my friends. I imagined bonfires, games, and camping. I decided I was willing to step outside my comfort zone if my best friends surrounded me. I couldn't wait to go.

We needed to sign a liability waiver stating that Camp Crescent Moon wasn't responsible for any injury suffered while on the premises. I never thought twice about that. My parents signed it, I shoved it into my backpack, and I forgot about it. By then, the anticipation of leaving for the trip was killing me.

One night after a baseball game, I realized I was leaving for the retreat in the morning. I procrastinated. I still had to go shopping for all the things I needed for the trip, and it was already nine o'clock. I was often disorganized back then; I'd lost my supply list. So for most things, I guessed. My mom took me shopping and helped me decide what I should buy. My thought process went something like this: *Okay, I'll be in the woods for a week. I need bug spray, a flashlight, and a water bottle, and I'll be good.* This approach worked pretty well as it often had in my life, but I missed one vital detail: I was supposed to buy a certain type of bug spray, one that repelled ticks and other infectious parasites.

The morning arrived, and I was on a two-hour bus ride with my friends heading toward a week of adventure. As the bus driver turned onto a bumpy dirt road, I knew we had arrived. I saw ten or so log cabins with porches, and I saw many totem poles, each carved with the image of a mythological figure. As the camp staff described to us throughout the next few days, each was symbolic of a different animal that in Native American belief would be with every human throughout his or her life. Every person has a spirit animal based on birth month and emulates it physically and spiritually.

Being raised in a Roman Catholic home, I felt a slight disconnect between my spiritual life and animals. My faith taught me that human beings were superior and separated from the natural world, that we have evolved above all other creatures. In school, I was taught that God made animals first before finally creating humans, the greatest of all His creations.

My time at Camp Crescent Moon introduced me to the idea that humans and animals join as one in nature. That brought me back to my childhood roots; I'd spent hours on the hiking trails near my Attleboro home. That was a calming sense, one that I embraced; it stuck with me through the following days.

The camp was covered in an array of trees and shrubbery that were about to bloom in the brisk, spring air. I could hear people singing camp songs—they were the counselors who were waiting to greet us. After getting situated in my cabin, I sat on my top bunk, giddy with anticipation of the week ahead. My best friend, Jarred, was below me. Our side of the cabin had four bunks seven of my friends and I shared. A hallway connected a second identical side of the cabin that also had four bunks.

That week, Jarred and I spent many nights talking after lights out. He and I could make two hours of conversation feel like just five minutes. He and I joked that we were encouraged to rough it while at camp though we were in a heated cabin with electricity and showers with hot water.

The first thing we did was have a meeting with the camp staff. One of the head counselors assured us we were in for a week of fun as long as we followed the rules and stayed safe. Every time we came in from outside, we needed to take our shoes and socks off and check ourselves for ticks, they said. *Sure*, I thought. *What's a bug going to do to me?* I never gave the warning a second thought.

It was a week of adventure—a week to play, a week to learn—a week I will never forget. From expeditious hikes to insect-anatomy classes, my week at the camp was full of experiences. We learned about nature and the importance of preserving life.

The first day was dull, rainy, and cold, but we still went on a hike to a spring-peeper pond. I heard all the spring peepers singing in unison, an almost deafening roar. Though this frog is about the size of a thumb, its decibel level is on par with an opera singer's. Hearing one of them sing was like being stuck in the eardrum by a needle, but when they were in unison, they created a calming and tranquil atmosphere—the antithesis of the civilized world.

After the hike, I saw the beauty in nature and realized the importance of the trip. Once my perspective changed, I viewed our activities differently. It was no longer a simple field trip but an existential journey. I pondered the sounds of nature and listened to my heart. I finally understood the meaning of this trip—to appreciate life through a different lens. I was lost in this meditative period for a while after the hike was over. All the students and counselors got together around a campfire. As I sat by myself admiring the beauty around me—the bark of the trees and sound of the wind—I felt a tap on my shoulder.

"Is everything okay?" I heard a pleasant voice ask.

"Yeah, I'm fine. I was just thinking," I said.

"I'm Gabby. I'm one of the counselors. Why don't you sit with us?"

She was the prettiest counselor at the camp, so I could hardly refuse.

"What's your name?" she asked.

"Pat."

She rifled through the papers on her clipboard. "Awesome! You're in my group."

"What do you mean?"

"Each counselor has a group of six students with whom we do all our activities."

I was smiling on the inside. "That's so cool."

"How do you like Crescent Moon so far?"

I struggled to find words because I didn't want to make a fool of myself in front of the prettiest counselor at camp and because words couldn't describe what I was feeling. "It's awesome" was the best I could do; it was as if I were finally at peace in my life.

She offered me a marshmallow, as we continued talking.

Every student and teacher from my middle school was at that gathering; we were learning to see and live differently. We sang songs and ate marshmallows while one counselor played guitar.

As the week continued, every morning we were reminded of ticks and told we should check ourselves often, but I treated that like the safety-procedure lecture on an airplane. At home, I saw ticks all the time on my dogs and occasionally on myself. I'd never been harmed in the past, so I thought this was no different. Throughout the week, I didn't check myself once. I suppose I was being defiant.

I was having the time of my life. We hiked the vast woods and picked up garbage along the highway. We spent a night in a tent under the stars. We fished for tadpoles in the murky ponds and saw what farm life was like. We learned to milk cows, churn butter, and sheer sheep.

My favorite part came during the last day—we ran an obstacle course full of many challenging activities that involved teamwork. I learned I needed to work with others to accomplish goals.

Gabby introduced our obstacle to the group—Tarzan—two platforms separated by a ten-foot pond below. The only way to get across was by way of a rope swing. We were instructed to go across. The six of us swung to the other side one by one with ease. When we made it to the other side, Gabby said, "Nice job, guys. Now the game begins."

We were confused.

"On the way back, only one of you can be on the rope swing. You need to work as a team to get everyone back to this side. You have five minutes."

I turned to my group. "Okay, so who wants to be Tarzan?" All five of my teammates pointed to me. I peered over the ledge into the muddy, swampy water and wondered how this was going to work. The idea of me freezing cold and dirty was my impetus to avoid a swampy plunge. I took the lightest girl piggyback, and we made it over without an issue. I swung back and retrieved the next team member. I was able to carry four of them over without an issue. However, Jackson was an issue; he was much taller than me. His legs wrapped around my body. As we swung, his boot got caught on the rope and fell into the water. We made it to the other side, but he was minus a boot.

Without missing a beat, I swung back over to try to retrieve his boot. On my first pass, I missed. The rope wasn't designed to touch the water, but I needed to manipulate it to be able to grab the boot. The boot was slowly drifting away. I swung for it at an angle. My leg and arm skimmed the water. I scooped his boot from the water in a great splash. I barely reached the platform, landed, and rolled. I was wet, his boot was safe, and I was a hero.

The week was finally over, which was bittersweet. I hadn't known how I would feel being away from my family for a week, but the time at camp taught me that I could be self-sufficient and more important that I had a core group of friends I could trust. I was upset that I had to leave. On the last day, I hugged Gabby and said good-bye to the camp I had grown to love. We boarded the bus and drove back to St. Stephan's, where my mom greeted me. She hugged me as though she'd never let go. I wasn't embarrassed; I embraced her love.

The next few weeks were life as usual until one day after school. While I was in the shower, I felt a lump on the back of my head. *That's strange.* I had hair down to my shoulders, though, so I thought it might just be a clump of dirt. I scratched at it to get it out, but it wouldn't come out. That's when I started to worry. I felt my stomach drop. My fear became real. I began frantically groping the back of my head trying to figure out what the mysterious lump was. Then I felt it move. I finally ripped it out and threw it on the shower floor. I looked beyond my bloodied hands at the shower drain. Crawling among a small mound of freshly extracted hair was a tick the size of a quarter. I had extracted the deeply seated insect from below my flesh—seemingly from my skull. The water on the floor of the shower instantly turned a vile, crimson red. I washed the tick down the drain.

I knew I was in trouble.

This was not like my encounters with ticks in the past when I effortlessly pulled them from my dog's fur. This was different. I vaguely remembered the warnings at Camp Crescent Moon. "A tick only has to be attached to you for forty-eight hours before spreading Lyme disease into your system," they'd said. That was way past forty-eight hours; it had been several weeks. I had hardly gone outside since I'd been home. I was certain the tick was from the camp. All the warnings I had previously ignored came to the center of my consciousness.

I was terrified and unsure what to do. I wanted to tell my dad—his niece, my cousin Sue, was a nurse practitioner specializing in Lyme disease. I dried myself off and found my dad. He was in his home office making some copies.

"Dad, I have a problem."

"What's wrong?"

"I found a tick on the back of my head."

"As long as it wasn't under your skin, you're okay."

It had been under my skin—deep under my skin, but I didn't want to tell my father that; I didn't want to alarm anyone. I was shaken by what my father had said, but I internalized my feelings. At that point in my life, I felt self-sufficient. *I have this under control. It was just tangled in my hair.*

Chapter 2
What's Happening to Me?

About a week after I found the tick, my nose and sinuses became congested. I didn't connect the two events, nor did anyone else. I had never been diagnosed with any allergies, but that seemed to be the only explanation for the sudden flare-up of congestion and fatigue. My parents gave me over-the-counter allergy medicine that helped take the edge off the congestion. I ignored my symptoms, fought through the congestion, and went to school.

But after I spent a week fighting the symptoms and struggling to stay attentive in school, my parents decided to take me to a doctor. That's when the web of confusion began to spread. *What's happening to me?* became a question I asked myself often.

My parents took me to my primary care physician, who diagnosed me with a sinus infection and prescribed antibiotics. After a week of taking those and resting, the congestion went away. Three days later, though, the congestion came back, and it was even more debilitating. My face swelled. My nose was three times its normal size. I could hardly function because of the pressure in my head. I was barely able to keep my eyes open because of the pressure above my brow. Every time I opened my mouth, I experienced excruciating pain in my face and neck. Phlegm coated the back of my throat and kept my ears blocked. I suffered a combination of pain; it was like having a sore throat and a violent head cold while being on an airplane. My ears being stuffed up hindered my listening and affected my balance. Every time I stood, I stumbled and was ungainly.

When I went back to the doctor, he dismissed my symptoms as

normal for a sinus infection. Because the phlegm in my throat prevented me from speaking any sentence longer than five words, it was impossible for me to communicate the full extent of my suffering to him. My parents told my doctors what I was going through; they could see I wasn't myself.

Even still, I was a kid, so I fought my problems trusting everything would be okay again soon. Throughout the next few weeks, I spent a good amount of time outside despite my fatigue and congestion. The hardest part of overcoming the symptoms was the first step. Once I began running, I felt almost like my old self. My chest was heavy and my balance a bit off, but I enjoyed myself. However, the first step was the hardest to make. Congestion made it difficult to breathe, and my balance was shaky at best. Even the slight effort it took to stand up from the couch left me out of breath and dizzy; those were the hardest moments. But once I got moving, I was myself. Running energized me and gave me something to look forward to. I decided to dedicate my energy to baseball, the sport I loved.

When my school year drew to a close two months later, I was still battling symptoms. I finished the year with a B average and perfect attendance. I figured I could recover from my ailment during the summer. I hung out with friends and played baseball, but the fatigue continued. I was lethargic all day every day. I was on antibiotics for sinus infections all summer but didn't improve.

My mom was diagnosed with stage 2 breast cancer, and I realized I wasn't the main priority. My mom's battle further incentivized me fight through my symptoms. *My mom is feeling much worse than I am. I can do this.* Still, all my friends had much more energy than I did. While at friends' houses, I was unable to participate as much as I wanted to. In between innings, instead of standing up and cheering my teammates, I sat on the bench gasping for air and closing my eyes for as long as possible before going back out onto the field.

That was when I started to feel different and socially isolated. One day, I was playing flag football. After about fifteen minutes of playing at a moderate pace, I felt I needed to sit down. I left the game to sit in the grass and watch for a while, but I ended up falling asleep. About an hour later, one of my friends woke me up to tell me it was time to leave.

None of my friends ever called me out for doing that; they assumed I was responding to the emotional burden of having a mother who was battling cancer and needed some time for myself. But my mom's battle was in the back of my mind. I was simply too physically exhausted to keep playing. That was the first time I felt I had truly missed out and the first time my condition controlled what I did.

The time I was not sleeping or playing baseball was limited. I kept to myself; life was easier that way. I didn't know how to fix what was happening or who could help me, so I pretended everything was fine. I didn't tell anyone what was really going on—not even my parents. My family was shaken by my mom's diagnosis, and I didn't want to add more stress. My parents noticed my fatigue and visible congestion, but they weren't aware of my emotional struggle and the isolation I was feeling that was affecting my self-confidence. Nonetheless, I felt that my struggle was mine to fight.

When I returned to school in the fall, I was still exhausted and congested. My parents and I concluded I must have had a problem much bigger than allergies. School became progressively difficult for me because I didn't feel well enough to do my work. I went back to my primary care physician.

"Aren't sinus infections supposed to go away?" I asked.

"Yes, they certainly should."

He referred us to an allergist. I was relieved; I felt I was a step closer to recovery. But my father and I were the only two who knew about the tick. Neither of us considered that it could have been the cause of my symptoms. *There's no way.*

The allergist gave me a prick test of 200 shots to test for every kind of allergen airborne or otherwise. I forgot about the pain of the needles and hoped I would have an answer after the test results came back. After being poked and prodded for what felt like forever, I had no kind of allergic reaction whatsoever. As I sat on the table in that office, I felt empty and confused about why I had no allergies. I was clueless about what to do next. I stared at the places where pricks were made and begged my body to react, but nothing came.

My family, my doctors, and I all believed I was allergic to something that was causing my congestion and fatigue. The allergist said there was definitely something wrong but didn't know what it was. I was nervous. The allergist wondered if it was a structural issue, something perhaps that was defective from my premature birth. A misshapen sinus? A malformed bone? He told us to go see an ear, nose, and throat doctor.

We went to an ENT, and she did some more tests, including taking X-rays and sticking a camera up my nose and through my sinuses as well as down my throat. These tests only exacerbated the pain I was feeling in my sinuses and provided me with false hope. They were not only invasive and painful but also inconclusive. After the maddening tests were completed, I remained without a diagnosis and without any other options. I had been battling sickness for about eight months and yet supposedly nothing was wrong with me. My aggravation began to surface; I was desperate to find out what was wrong with me. I became increasingly short-tempered.

One day when my dad picked me up from school, I hopped into his car and buckled up. As he did every day, he asked, "How was your day?"

"Why do you care? Honestly?" I shot back. "You ask me the same question every single day, and every day I say I feel horrible! What made you think today would be any different?"

My dad knew I needed to cool off, so he softly uttered, "I'm sorry."

These were not just the words of a hormonal preteen; they were inspired by frustration. I was plagued by an illness. I knew something else was wrong.

The initial diagnosis, a sinus infection, seemed less and less likely. My sinuses were inflamed, but my congestion wasn't caused by mucus. When I would blow my nose, nothing would come out. Even prescription nasal sprays couldn't alleviate my congestion.

My mom brought me to another primary care physician. "I'm sure she'll know what's wrong and make you feel better," she said.

During the appointment, I was sure we were getting nowhere.

"Have you tried Nasonex?"

"Yes."

"What about Nasacort?"

"Yes."

"How about Rhinocort?"

My mom interjected, "Yes, and Flonase and Dymista and every other spray over the counter or prescription."

The doctor looked at me almost pleadingly.

"And none of them helped your congestion?"

"No! They make it worse."

"That's very unfortunate. Umm ... I'll have you try Nasacort again."

I wanted to scream. I knew nasal sprays didn't help. I'd tried them all. My parents and I knew it wasn't allergies.

The ENT was convinced something had gone wrong with the series of tests I'd had at the allergist, so we went back. The allergist guessed it was a pubescent onset of allergies, but he never found any. He stopped answering my parents' calls. After my parents had pestered his receptionist for several weeks, he finally called to tell them that he didn't know what was wrong with me and that they should take me to another doctor.

I knew my case was complicated; it had stumped four doctors. That was unnerving. My parents and I had no guide on this journey for a cure. Though we didn't have the medical support we needed, my parents stayed by my side. They valiantly searched for a doctor who could help me. Despite my ambiguous malady, I kept my faith. I began to pray to God, "Please give these doctors knowledge to help me." That gave me some assurance, but still, I'd never heard a doctor say, "I don't know" before. That, however, was becoming a pattern.

Until that point, the sages in white coats had easily cured any ailment that couldn't be solved with bedrest. My sense of security was taken from me when I discovered that my safety net was more porous than I had thought. This was when I realized I couldn't always be protected. I'd had a similar false sense of security growing up as well. As a child, I'd felt most secure in my house with my parents. On the rare occasions that my parents were unable to protect me, I prayed to God for protection. As my battle continued, my parents were always by my side, but they could do almost nothing to protect me.

The ENT sent the referral back to the allergist, and after several weeks, once again we visited the allergist. My head was spinning as I stumbled into the waiting room. That time, he offered a remedy: an antidepressant. He said all my symptoms were psychosomatic. I'd had no experience with depression; I was sure it wasn't the cause of my ailments. That frustrated me even more. Instead of solving my unusual case, doctors preferred to protect their own credibility.

In spite of my debilitating symptoms and social isolation, I remained optimistic. Before that time, I'd never been happier. I was hopeful for the future, being cured, and returning to life as normal. I viewed this period of persistent symptoms as a speed bump on the superhighway of my life. There was not a legitimate issue that the doctor or anyone else could physically see, so he played it off as an emotional issue. At that point, I didn't know what to believe. My parents decided not to follow his advice. They believed his recommendation was as ludicrous as I did. His lack of sympathy and understanding made my skin crawl.

One of the most frustrating things I have ever been through was having symptoms rule my life and being unable to express the full extent to which they were incapacitating me and having no one but my parents believe me.

Determined to find an answer, my parents brought me to a different doctor almost every week. Every time I went to a new doctor, my parents spent about twenty minutes reciting my medical and symptom history. Nearly every time, the doctors sent me for blood tests, additional medical examinations, and psychological evaluations. Most of the time at the follow-up appointments, I was sent out of the room—presumably to protect my innocence, but I could hear the conversation through the wall. On several occasions, I heard a muffled, pseudo-compassionate voice saying, "There's nothing wrong with him. I'm sorry, I just can't help you. It's all in his head."

My parents would ask, "What should we do?"

That was followed by a long, painful silence and a recommendation that I see another doctor.

My chronic symptoms and the doubts of the doctors left me bitter. I began asking myself, *Why me?* I grew contemptuous of everyone, including my friends and family, simply because they were healthy and I wasn't. I became jealous of my classmates. In the classroom, I had to control my frustration when other students were bubbly and lively; I struggled to stay awake. I hoped one of my other classmates would not complete assignments or not do well on tests so I wouldn't have the lowest grade in the class anymore. Realizing that praying for a cure wasn't a solution, I began to pray that others would experience my pain. I thought, *If only anyone else understood how I was feeling, maybe they'd care.* It was a dark period for me when I started wishing my symptoms on others. In my mind and in my life, my illness was shifting from mild, bearable, and temporary to debilitating and unending. I went to an herbalist, chiropractor, and even a hypnotist to no avail. The only thing that was certain: whatever I was experiencing was anything but normal.

My primary care physician retired, which left us alone in our search for a cure. We had no reference point and no idea of what to do next. My parents were still at my side, rosary beads clutched and praying for an answer. They knew I wasn't faking my symptoms. They experienced my daily struggle. I was beginning to lose faith, but I still uttered a prayer for a cure every once in a long while.

On a practical level, without a primary care referral, it was nearly impossible to get appointments with other doctors. This landed me in my pajamas, sleeping in yard-sale chairs in the unfinished waiting rooms of underqualified, inexperienced practitioners. It seemed as though we had no one on our side, but even worse, no one who believed me. "There's nothing wrong with you," they all said. I was fading away from the person I once was; those words penetrated my very being and sucked the life out of me even more than my unidentified illness had. I began to lose hope for recovery.

My middle school didn't understand the profound impact my illness had on my ability to function; my parents began to see my chronic symptoms as my new normal. The only person who had any sort of compassion for my illness was my cousin, Auntie Sue, as I call her. At several family gatherings during this period of struggle, I overheard Sue talking to my family members, trying to convince them that Lyme disease caused many of the medical problems they were complaining about. For this, she was dubbed "The crazy Lyme lady."

Crazy or not, Sue understood what it was like to be told nothing was wrong with her. Only she empathized with my suffering and didn't think I was faking. She'd had Lyme disease for ten years and had gotten fed up with all the doctors not having a clue about what was wrong with her. For that reason, she'd put herself through school to become a nurse practitioner who specialized in Lyme disease. She encouraged me to be tested for Lyme. My parents brushed this off. Sue knew what she was talking about, but she seemed to think everything was Lyme disease. And she had just started her practice and hadn't seen any patients. My parents appreciated her concern, but they knew there had to be someone who knew what was wrong with me. Even though Sue is one of our closest family members, my parents were adamant about taking me to a "real" doctor.

Lack of diagnosis aside, Sue lifted my spirits with her whimsical humor. She always found a way to make me smile. She treated me just like everyone else though I felt far from normal. She treated me like a normal kid while I was fading into oblivion.

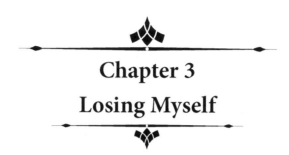

Chapter 3
Losing Myself

After months of trying to find out what was wrong with me, I wasn't myself anymore. I could no longer concentrate because of the pressure in my head. The sinuses behind my forehead felt like they were going to explode, and my face was scrunched up like a pit bull's. Despite the pressure, I felt light-headed, scattered, and forgetful.

I continued to go to school feeling half-dead, and I pretty much was. I was usually late because of the awful fatigue. In the mornings, my dad had to practically drag me out of bed. Even if I did eventually wake up, pull myself together, and get into the shower, it was not uncommon for me to fall asleep in the shower standing up. I was never a great student, but at that time, I was struggling to stay afloat. For the majority of seventh grade, I sat in the back of my classes staring off into space. All I wanted to do was sleep.

I routinely dozed off during class. My mind was foggy, and my thoughts were unclear. My already sloppy handwriting turned into scribbles. My word recognition and reading skills were almost nonexistent—that scared me, but I was so lost I didn't say anything. I didn't know what to do, and it seemed that no one would or could help. I was failing multiple classes and was barely scraping by in the others, but I didn't care.

My classmates probably thought I was on drugs, and at that point, I wished I had been. I had hardly any friends because they all thought I'd gone crazy given my perpetual catatonic state.

One day at recess, one classmate said, "Let's play football."

"No, we always play that," came the response from another.

"How about wall ball?"

"Ultimate Frisbee?"

I said, "Let's … umm …" I couldn't find my words.

My friends were staring at me.

I tried it again. "Let's play …" I couldn't remember what I was going to say for a few seconds. "Four-square."

"You're so socially awkward," a girl said.

The group burst into laughter.

I didn't know how to respond. I shrugged and said, "I don't know," being even more awkward.

They played wall ball. I sat by myself.

With no diagnosis, no medication, and no one who believed me, I felt alone—even separated from myself—while I battled the biggest fight of my life.

As always, my parents remained at my side. On the car rides home from school, I frequently discussed my pain with my father. I told him I couldn't stand going to school and being embarrassed in front of all of my friends anymore. My pride was hurt when I had to admit I was unable to do the things I used to be able to do, but my dad encouraged me to keep fighting. My parents had always taught me to always try my best; that's all that mattered. But my best wasn't good enough anymore.

That was when the feeling of helplessness truly set in. In the classroom during our downtime, as the other kids were socializing, I was literally kicked out of the inner circle. As my classmates would talk in a circle, they were so tightly situated that it was clear there was no room for me. I could halt conversations by simply approaching my peers. My presence shifted the mood of my conversing classmates from jocular to solemn. Some of my best friends turned their backs on me. I began eating lunch by myself immersed in my thoughts. *Why is this happening to me? I thought they were my friends.*

I had always been frustrated with my parents for being on my back, but being sick with no diagnosis showed me they were the only ones who ever had my back. My parents defended me during my fight when I became unable to defend myself. They showed their unconditional love for me through their perseverance to find a cure and by constantly taking me to new doctors.

I was perpetually uneasy. I have only a vague recollection of that period—I was so sick, and there were too many doctors to remember. It was a fog of waiting rooms, with me half-asleep on my dad's shoulder. Despite our valiant efforts, I was getting sicker and sicker.

A new symptom rose seemingly out of nowhere: claustrophobia. It began one day while I was in the bathroom preparing for a family party. I couldn't button the top button on my shirt because of my swollen glands, so my dad offered some assistance. He got down on a knee and attempted to feed the top button through the hole. My dad took hold of the collar and pulled it just slightly tighter. I pushed him away. I couldn't breathe. He put his hand on my shoulder.

"Pat? What's wrong?"

I slapped his hand away. "Don't touch me!" I felt trapped. I grasped my chest as I started to hyperventilate. I began to slide down the wall thinking, *I'm going to die.* Then a switch flipped. I had a meltdown, a fight-or-flight reaction; I felt that I was fending for my life. I fell to the floor writhing and screaming. My ears pounded to the beat of my heart. I struck my fists against the cool blue tile. My dad attempted to console me, but that only exacerbated the situation. He was closing me in even more. I had to get out of there. I began to punch and kick him as I sprung to my feet. I pushed the Plexiglas panel from the shower, and as it fell to the floor, so did I.

When I hit the floor for the second time, I became calmer; I was no longer angry. I was crying softly. I grabbed the sink and pulled myself to my feet. I leaned on the sink and stared into the mirror at my reddened, teary eyes. When my dad hugged me, I became violent. "Let me out of here!" I shoved him away and did a swim move to get around him. I stomped across the hallway into my bedroom and flung myself on my bed. I assumed the fetal position and cried. My dad walked in. I softly said, "Don't touch me. Please don't touch me" repeatedly until I fell asleep. I didn't go to the party.

Several hours later, I awoke and had a similar panic attack when I saw the ceiling and walls of my room only inches from me. This newfound symptom presented itself in other ways as well. At my routine appointments, I was no longer able to take the elevator. Despite arthritic joints and trembling hands, I grasped the metal railings and climbed what seemed like endless flights of stairs in medical buildings. I kept one hand on the railing and the other pushing on my knees forcing them to move.

When this new symptom surfaced, and when we were pretty much out of options, one of our family friends, a nephrologist, offered some assistance He was my grandparents' neighbor and was almost like extended family, so he was determined to get to the bottom of my illness.

Even though he didn't specialize in diagnostics, he had a more significant pull in the medical community than we did. He ran a litany of tests—an EKG, several EEGs, blood tests, MRIs, CT scans, and blood tests for every imaginable disease including Lyme disease—in search of a diagnosis, especially for a cause of my new symptom. Each test came back negative or inconclusive. Then even our family friend was out of options. Stumped by my case. Again the question, *Is this all in my head?*

My physical state was abysmal, but my emotional state was even worse. I wished I were dead since that was how I felt anyway. On top of the fatigue were migraine headaches, joint aches, and worst of all, the anger. I was angry at everything and everybody; it seemed like no one cared what was wrong with me. There were nights I would lie in bed and say, "If there is a God, please kill me before I kill myself so I'm not a burden on my family anymore."

I had always attended Catholic schools, but that was the first time I had actually questioned the existence of God. I was challenging God and asking Him to prove Himself to me by taking my life. This marked the shift in my relationship with God, whom I had believed to be the mightiest of all powers—it transformed from unconditional love to justifiable hate. He had not listened to my prayers for my Uncle Brad, nor had he listened to those for my recovery.

Feeling neglected and burdensome, I fell away from my family too. Everything my family did revolved around how I felt. If I had one of my fits of rage or a claustrophobia attack, my family was unable to leave the house for fear of leaving me alone. They had to stay with me for my safety, not theirs. I drained my family's time for appointments and money for copays, and I took my aggression out on them physically.

During these episodes, I lost emotional attachment to whoever was around me and attacked anyone who moved. My fog of pain permeated my being, and I transferred my pain onto them.

I went to school every day and moped around indignantly. No longer feeling like myself, I decided to roll over. I pretended I didn't exist; wishful thinking, I suppose. I felt no need for friends, nor did I have any. All the friends I had prior to my inexplicable illness had abandoned me. That made me think about what kind of people my friends really were. Social isolation in school turned into unanswered phone calls and text messages and eventually into them ignoring me completely.

The rejection from my peers only exacerbated my emotional distress. That led to violent outbursts—my anger had been an increasing problem, but it then moved from frustration to rage. The outbursts ranged from cussing out my parents and throwing things to having complete meltdowns and screaming my head off in the middle of the road at two in the morning. My family was careful not to set me off. Any sudden change of plans or frivolous thing that didn't go my way prompted a violent tantrum. Usually, if I was tired and my parents asked me to extend myself or do something that I didn't want to do, I'd blow up.

Once during the winter, despite below-freezing weather and a foot of snow, I was outside shooting hoops to get my mind off my situation. When my sister Alicia came home late at night from an evening with friends, she saw me at the end of the driveway and began honking her horn and flashing her high beams. She stopped the car and waved at me like a moron just to say "Hello!" I was startled by the sudden noise and was overcome by rage. I heaved my basketball at her windshield. She screamed, "What's wrong with you?" I cursed at her loud enough for the entire neighborhood to hear. After she told my parents, my dad came out to comfort me. At the sight of him, I exploded. Knowing he had come to console me, I transferred the rage I felt toward my sister onto him.

Innocuous changes were my triggers. One day several weeks later at around one in the morning, I woke up from a nap that had started the previous day. I stumbled into the bathroom, my head spinning and joints aching. While turning the shower on, I realized my shampoo was missing. I knew instantly that one of my sisters had taken it because I knew my parents wouldn't have been so "cruel."

I stormed upstairs to my sisters' bathroom and searched for my shampoo. I didn't find it, so I went into my sister Mikaela's room, opened the door, and began to swear at her and screamed, "Where's my shampoo?" Before she could muster an answer from her sleepy state, I flipped on the light in her room and tore it apart in search of the "stolen" shampoo.

My mother had heard the commotion and came into the room asking what was going on. I felt trapped and flustered by the situation and began to panic. I felt confined in my sister's room and in my house. So at two in the morning, I ran outside and to the end of our street. About ten minutes later, my mom drove up the street looking and calling for me out the car window as if searching for a lost dog. She eventually found me writhing and screaming on the asphalt.

When these fits of rage happened, I went into the "zone," as if my entire mind shut off and focused only on killing everyone and everything around me. Rage pulsed through my veins during these tantrums, and I had no concern for anything. I even struck family members. I forgot all emotional connections I had to those who got in my way. I was out of control, even throwing dishes and upturning tables. However, after every outburst, I always ended up breaking down crying.

After about six months of uncontrollable anger, my parents began to believe psychosis was my only diagnosis, and they took me to a therapist. Though they saw my symptoms and experienced the fallout and though they didn't want to admit they didn't believe me, my parents began to believe that my real problem was rage.

One day, after my dad picked me up from school, he said I had a doctor's appointment, which of course seemed ordinary at that point. When my dad pulled into the parking lot, I realized he was taking me to a talk therapist. I lost it. I ran around the parking lot screaming and crying, "I'm not crazy!" I was belligerent and full of rage. (But a sane person does not usually run around a parking lot frantically sobbing and striking parked cars.) My dad locked the car, so I pounded on the glass and knocked off one of the side-view mirrors.

After several minutes of running and striking my dad's car, I was tired and calmed down. I had my first of many unproductive sessions with that therapist. She told me her purpose was to help control my anger. I was constantly frustrated with the therapist because she didn't understand what I was feeling—because no one else could ever truly understand. As we addressed all the medical and social struggles I was dealing with, she continued to ask, "How does that make you feel?" in a stereotypical, monotone, and apathetic therapist's voice. During our appointments, though, and all other times when I was not having one of my tantrums, I was soft spoken and composed. In my typical state, I didn't even recall my episodes of rage; it was as if they had never happened. Whenever a family member brought up the subject, I became frustrated and threw a fit.

My therapist encouraged me to spend what little energy I had on my schoolwork and not on outbursts. If it had been my choice, I would have followed her advice. After a few months with her, I hated her more than I thought humanly possible; I'd tell her how I really felt and what went through my head, and she recommended I be put on antidepressants. This was her informed conclusion after examining the workings of my brain and dark thoughts. It seemed that she too believed that my symptoms were all in my head.

The epitome of frustration is speaking and not being understood. I felt she was avoiding the real issue. My outbursts had begun only after I'd gotten sick. It was as if I had duct tape over my mouth and was incapable of expressing my situation to her. I belonged at school playing with my friends, not in her office being prescribed antidepressants. Even my parents thought her suggestion was extreme; they knew I was emotionally drained only because of my constant symptoms. We never went to see her again—but that was not the last time I would see a therapist.

My parents began to grapple with the possibility that I was mentally ill. But they knew my mental issues were not their only concern, and they continued to seek alternate routes. Though my parents never fully lost faith in what I was telling them, that was a time when their belief in me faltered.

Underneath all the turmoil, anger, and fatigue, I wished everything could go back to the way it had been. I had hoped I could wake up one day feeling like my old self again, but after almost a year of misery, lethargy had become my new normal, aches and pains were ubiquitous, and suicidal thoughts were just background noise. I lost belief in my own recovery, and my parents were beginning to give up on me. I forgot about God, and I seemed to have only one friend who hadn't given up on me.

Chapter 4
A Reprieve from the Pain

Despite my emotional and physical symptoms, I found motivation to keep pushing forward: I began a school science project with my best friend Jarred Lorrusso. Jarred was one of the few people who didn't leave me during my time of need. Both of us were twelve and years away from driving, but we came up with the idea of building a full-scale, drivable electric car.

With much help from our science teacher and our families, we successfully converted a gas-powered 1998 Saturn into a fully electric car. We set the standard of achievement at a school for overachievers. We were the best of the best. However, I didn't believe it because of my chronic symptoms. When I was healthy, this description fit me perfectly; I'd always done everything to the best of my ability. This included sports, school, and life in general. But even the sick version of me had an overachiever lurking inside. And I'm a fighter, so the overachiever—the scrappy, hard-working kid—found a way out. Even though it was exceedingly difficult to work on the car, I did it because the work gave me purpose. I don't know if I could've made it without that inborn tenacity, my friend Jarred, and that project to take my mind off how out of control my life was.

When it was time for our annual science project, my science teacher, Mr. Mongillio, told our class about the Macari fund—a fund designated for green energy projects. He told us there was a wide variety of projects to choose from, that we could do a solar-powered oven, a hydrogen-powered model car, a hovercraft, or (as he showed us a book titled *How to Build an Electric Car*), a full-size electric car.

Mr. Mongillio was showing us that big projects such as those were possible. By virtue of him saying that with conviction, I knew he believed students could successfully do such an ambitious project. I knew I was up for the challenge; it would be my way to feel like myself again, to feel alive again. It caught my imagination and gave me hope and a sense of excitement. I felt this project was the perfect opportunity to express my ingenuity and overall creativity. So after class, I told Mr. Mongillio, "Mr. M, I want to build an electric car."

He chuckled. "Patrick, you know I wasn't entirely serious when I brought up the electric car."

"But I seriously want to do it."

He seemed ambivalent and continued to explain that as a former professor, he had overseen several gas-to-electric car conversions. "It takes roughly a hundred hours of labor to do the conversion. It would be a part-time job for you. Plus, there will be many expenses probably not covered by the Macari fund."

I didn't care about obstacles; I knew I'd find a way for it to work. I was sick of people doubting me, and I wanted to prove it.

"I'm up for the challenge if you are," I said.

Mr. M was almost as excited as I was. He set up a meeting with the administration.

The next day, I was pulled out of my first class and into a meeting with Sr. Renee, the principal, Dr. Conlin, the vice principal, and Mr. Mongillio.

"So I hear you have quite the project planned," Sr. Renee said.

I laughed. "Yes, I do."

"What's your plan?" she asked.

"I want to do just what the book says—make an electric car. Obviously, I'll need a lot of help, but I really want to do it. Mr. M said that he has done these projects before, so he can be a mentor."

"We want to make sure you'll be dedicated to this before we make the investment," Sr. Renee said.

I nodded. "I'm very excited about doing this. I really care about the environment and preventing global warming. This is a project I'll work really hard on."

Their expressions told me that was exactly what they had wanted to hear.

"We know you're a good student," Dr. Conlin said, "so we know you'll take this project seriously." His elbows were on the table. He opened his hands, pointed at me, and said, "I believe you can do it."

Sr. Renee smiled pleasantly and clasped her hands. "It seems like you've done well during your two years here. I'm glad you're finally finding something you're passionate about." She seemed relieved. "We'll give you the money from the Macari fund to help pay for it."

I was elated. "Thank you so much! I really appreciate it." I shook their hands.

"We know you won't let us down," Dr. Conlin said.

I knew I wouldn't.

Because they hadn't been in the classroom with me, they were oblivious to my symptoms. As far as they knew, I was the happy and healthy student they had always known. I felt empowered. I was taking back a piece of my old self. Science had always been my favorite subject. Ever since I could remember, I'd been mixing different household cleaners just to see what happens. I begged my parents on Saturdays to take me to the science museum while other children were playing video games. Science always intrigued me because it taught me about life. Not the *why* of life answered in my theology classes but the *how*. I was tired of asking "Why?" I was tired of wondering why all of these things were happening to me and wondering why I felt so poorly. I was tired of being tired, tired of lying around lethargically all day, and tired of lying to myself, saying that I had no hope.

I still had that fighter pent up inside like an enraged animal ready to come out. It was time to stop asking "Why?" and "Why me?" and to start asking "How?" *How can I change my situation? How can I make my life and the lives of those around me better? How can I make the best of my situation? How can I take the tools I have and use them to help others?* I was tired of moaning and complaining, and so I began to utilize the few skills I did still have and not worry about those I'd seemingly lost. My mind was altered, but I could still think creatively.

The next weekend I was at Jarred's; we were going to play paintball at the lumberyard owned by his father's construction company. In the midst of laughing and playing, I saw a massive building with a sign on the front that read "Lorrusso Garage." On the way back to Jarred's, I asked Mr. Lorrusso about his garage.

"It's where my mechanics service my cars and construction equipment," he said. I told him and Jarred about the electric car idea, and they were immediately all in.

The following Monday, I told Mr. M the good news: we had the help we needed for the project. He was ecstatic. He was ready to get started as quickly as we could because this was the biggest project he had ever done with kids our age. He reminded us it would not be easy and that we had our work cut out for us.

In the weeks that followed, we started searching for the perfect car. My father worked for a small business lending company that loaned to many used-car dealerships and had many contacts in that industry. We viewed at least a hundred cars: some were too big, some too old, some rusted out, some too new, and some out of our price range. Plus, the electric motor would work only with pre-2000 models because the car had to have limited computer involvement and a manual transmission. If the chassis was too large, the electric engine wouldn't be able to power it.

One day in the fall of 2009, my dad and I found the perfect car—a green 1998 Saturn, and it was even more perfect because its color matched our "green energy" project. The fact that it had over 250,000 miles on the engine was irrelevant because the engine would be removed and replaced with a new battery-driven one. The car cost $3,200, which was a little over the budget, but thanks to a generous donation from my father and Mr. Lorrusso, we were able to purchase the car that would soon be emission-free.

Within a few days, we had set a day to start; we agreed on Saturday at 8:00 a.m. I woke up that morning at nine feeling exhausted, achy, and worse than I'd felt before I went to bed. In spite of my fighting spirit, fatigue was the one thing I couldn't fight through. I had gone to bed around ten the night before and should have had no problem waking up. But I woke up more congested and fatigued than I thought possible. When I got to the garage at 9:30, I said I was late because of a doctor's appointment. This was the first lie I would tell about my illness.

I didn't want anyone to know I wasn't feeling well because I felt I'd bring everyone's mood down. Jarred and his father were aware of my illness, but unintentionally, the first impression I gave the mechanics was that I was a typical lazy teenager. In the following months, "I had a doctor's appointment" became a euphemism for "I was sleeping."

Despite my tardiness that day, we still accomplished many of the necessary preliminary tasks. The smell of rancid engine oil and the deafening sound of power tools set my head spinning. As always, once I began moving, I was able to complete work even though I felt fatigued. I assisted in stripping all unneeded parts such as the muffler system, gas tank, and engine. That took us about six hours. It was well worth it, though, when I stumbled back, looked through glassy eyes, and realized this outlandish project was really happening.

It took about a year and over a hundred man-hours—many from the mechanics—to finish the car. For that year, the entirety of our weekends was devoted to the conversion of the car. This was no small task for a thirteen-year-old battling an illness. I was using power tools, blowtorches, and working with batteries with enough voltage to kill us all instantly.

After removing all of the old parts and installing the new engine, we fabricated the metal boxes for each of the twenty-two batteries. The work was physically demanding on top of fighting my illness. I trudged through those weekends half-asleep. One day, we were installing a rack in the trunk to hold all the batteries I folded down the backseat to access the place. I lay down to reach a bolt. As I was lying there ratcheting in the bolt, I felt I never wanted to get up. When I finished ratcheting bolts in, I clawed my way out of the backseat and staggered to my feet. I leaned into the side of the car and put my head down into my forearms. This project seemed to be pushing me through my symptoms.

One day, we were carrying parts in that had been delivered. After carrying one forty-pound battery, I felt dizzy. I went to the bathroom and sat on the floor to rest for a bit. After that year of fighting excruciating pain in my joints, back, and neck, the electric car was fully operational. The electric vehicle got about forty miles to a charge and cruised comfortably on the highway.

But through the glory of the process and completion of the project,

I mostly remember being sick. I felt I hadn't contributed as much as I should or could have, and to this day, I feel guilty that because of my ailment, Jarred put in ten times the work I did. Jarred assured me that considering my circumstances, I contributed as much as I could, including our fifty-slide PowerPoint presentation, which depicted every step in the process.

Jarred (left) and I (right) showing the electric car during a publicity day.

The ensuing media surge was astonishing. The administration at St. Stephan's issued a press release and contacted all the major news stations in the area to inform them about the presentation. On January 22, 2010, the day of the presentation, at least twenty reporters from five TV stations and a number of newspapers came from all over New England to cover the story. We ended up on the front pages of three newspapers and the cover of *Autoweek* magazine. After the presentation, we were congratulated with a standing ovation, and then we gave everyone a tour of the car.

Once I'd appeared on local and national television, I was recognized everywhere. Many people I didn't know would approach me in public and question me about the car. Strangers always recognized me on the street and commended me for my efforts. I even took a few pictures and signed a few autographs. I received various awards for my ingenuity from the mayor of Attleboro as well as a citation from the Rhode Island senate.[2]

Though I continued to struggle with my undiagnosed illness, that euphoric time and all the publicity lifted my spirits enough to motivate me to continue fighting. The time seemed to go by so quickly, but it was the highlight of my life up to that point, and I was proud.

The plan was that after the car was finished, we would sell it at the annual St. Stephan's auction. Instead, the parents of our classmates pitched in and bought the car for Mr. Mongillio. He still drives the car to school every day. The car was registered to my father. We just needed to sign it over to Mr. M.

I'd just completed one of the most notable things in my life. I was proud and hopeful again. I felt a sense of relief; I was convinced my trying times were over.

Chapter 5
Back to Real Life

Looking back on the some of the TV interviews now, I see my former self—an exhausted person with visible facial congestion. Every word I said was labored, muffled by what sounded like a sore throat. My eyes were sunken, and I had dark circles under them.

The journalists and reporters did an outstanding job of bringing the story of the electric car to the public eye, but none of it—not what reporters said, what I said, or what my parents or doctors were saying—told my true story. It was a story no one wanted to hear, not even me. Behind the limelight, I suffered beyond measure. I was bedridden, but I was portrayed on television as an innovative, charismatic teenager.

It didn't make sense to me or anyone else. On paper, I was perfectly healthy. In the public eye, I was an overachiever, but behind closed doors, I was slowly dying. I had never felt worse than I had during that time, but I concealed my symptoms. Who I pretended to be during those interviews was not who I really was. I was living a secret life. I was finally somebody again even though I was pretending to be somebody else. I'd helped head up a successful project, but I was failing in school. My only focus had been the electric car as I hadn't cared much about anything else.

As I tried to balance these opposing thoughts, the same thought played over and over in my head: *There's nothing wrong with you.* But how could that be? Every time I had that thought, I became more certain something was wrong. I was chronically ill with sinus infections, back pain, memory loss, arthritic symptoms, emotional outbursts, and fatigue. Though others told me those things weren't happening, I knew they were. My doctors continued to tell me my symptoms weren't real because the only visible symptom they could see was the congestion. When my parents gave them detailed stories of my mood swings and emotional outbursts and lethargy, their only response was a subtle raise of an eyebrow as though they were thinking, *Are you serious?* I felt everyone was writing my symptoms off as laziness, thinking *He's a teenager*; I could see it in their eyes.

After several weeks, the buzz about the electric car wore down. I was no longer treated as a celebrity but as a normal kid. The distraction the car had provided me was gone, and I tried to avoid my illness in every way—I didn't talk about it, I tried not to think about it, and I made no attempt to get better. Schoolwork was nearly impossible, but my teachers gave me much more leniency than they did other students based on my accomplishments. I used this to avoid as much schoolwork as possible. I missed at least one day of school a week, and I was late the other four days for the remainder of the year. Other times, I took off full weeks. The physical symptoms were entirely debilitating. My back hurt so much that I couldn't move. Every muscle in my back felt perpetually knotted.

My life did have a bit of a pattern: I found out that the quality of my week was based on how I felt on Monday morning. If I was able to wake up and get to school, I knew it would be a bearable week. The sign of a bad week usually began on Sunday nights. Something as simple as my parents asking me to do my homework or asking where I wanted to go out for dinner would send me into a belligerent tantrum. Sobbing and hoarse from screaming, I'd eventually fall asleep surrounded by the destruction I had created in my room—it was as if I'd regressed to infancy. After these outbursts, I was thoroughly exhausted, so my parents didn't even try to wake me up in the morning.

Fighting against my fatigue and sickness got harder. After flunking every math test in the first quarter of seventh grade, I decided to stop trying. My problems stretched beyond simple exhaustion: I couldn't bring the shapes and numbers into visual focus. I had no idea why a shape looked different every time I tried to focus on it. I thought I was going insane; for me, circles were triangles and squares were diamonds. In algebra, with the added letter values, I saw letters as numbers and numbers as shapes. But I'd faced so much resistance before when asking for help that I didn't tell anyone. I knew no one would believe me. No one would care.

I could no longer read because I couldn't clearly see the words on the page. But according to the results of the eye exam administered by the school, I had perfect vision. Other times, I would be reading and hear voices in my head telling me crazy things. These voices born of my negative self-confidence provoked my anger and frustration. They said all the things I assumed my classmates were saying behind my back—*You're so stupid. Are you retarded? You're so fucking lazy.* When the voices weren't nagging me, I had constant ringing in my ears.

I abandoned my former fighting, driven self and developed a new coping strategy. Instead of facing my problems head-on, I became the class clown. I found it amusing and almost titillating to see how poorly I could do on a test just so my classmates would get a kick out of it. I played off my legitimate cognitive issues as some kind of innocuous and intentional action.

In my English class one day, my favorite teacher, Mr. Page, returned our spelling tests from the week before. The boy next to me read my failing grade and laughed. One word he found particularly amusing was *necessary.* I'd spelled it *nesedry.* An uproar of laughter ensued after the boy announced the mistake to the entire class while I sat in my seat quietly and thinking, *But that's how you spell it.* I thought I was losing my mind—and maybe I was. I was fine with amusing my friends with my failing grades when I intentionally tried to fail. But there was a bigger issue—I had actually been trying my best in English. My stomach dropped. Heat coursed throughout my body as my heart began to race. I was the laughingstock of the class.

When I lost my ability to write, my teachers contacted my parents. They thought I felt I was too good for their classes because of my recent achievements. But I simply couldn't do the things other students could. My hands were frail and nearly crippled, and I had purple bruises on my knuckles. The only thing I could do was scribble and pretend everything was okay.

I was sure I was sick, but my doubts about everything else ran deep. What kind of so-called loving God would make me so sick for so long?

Chapter 6
A Year Later, A Year Worse

By spring, I was missing between two and five days of school a week. In April of seventh grade, the middle school was getting ready to go back to Camp Crescent Moon for the yearly field trip. My debilitating symptoms grew only worse, so my doctors and parents advised me to stay home from the trip.

I spent the field trip week sleeping and imagining everything I was missing out on. I was prescribed antibiotics for yet another sinus infection. For the first time in months, I was on antibiotics again but was still somehow sicker than ever. I was bedridden that entire week. The sinus infection and my congestion got only worse. I slept nearly seventy hours in one three-day stretch. I could hardly move my mouth, even to talk or eat, because I was so congested. In an attempt to get rid of my congestion, I blew my nose nonstop, but nothing came out. I would eat, drink, go to the bathroom, and use my neti pot, a pour-through nasal rinsing device, but to no avail.

Though I was awake, I was far from coherent. My parents brought food to my room and forced me to eat and drink. I crawled to the bathroom and spent a few hours sleeping on the floor because I didn't have the strength to get back into bed. As I lay there, I felt numb, as if I were living in a dream. I heard noises in the house, but nothing could pull me from that sleep.

In an effort once again to discover the cause of the congestion, I went to a different allergist, and I told him my symptoms. The allergist gave the same diagnosis: he said it was an ear, nose, and throat issue. We told him we had already seen the ENT (as well as another allergist) and she had said it was definitely allergies. Dumbfounded, he sent me on my way with no answer.

My absence from Camp Crescent Moon that week gave me time to ponder all that had changed during the past year. I again questioned the existence of God. I didn't want to live that way anymore. I went from having all I could have ever asked for to being in circumstances I never asked for or wish on my worst enemy. I slipped back into wondering, *Why does this have to happen to me?* I indignantly asked these questions of God as if He had intentionally put me in my situation. I began to wonder if the doctors were right and all of this was in my head. I questioned the legitimacy of my symptoms and quickly realized they weren't anything I would or even could fake.

A few weeks after my classmates returned from camp, my friend Chris's actions were noticeably different. He had been cheerful and outgoing before the trip, but after his return, he became pensive and sullen. He developed an allergy to wheat. He hardly ever talked and seemed to not care about school. Once one of the smartest kids in my class, Chris was struggling immensely just to keep up. He was absent for more than two weeks, and he had a difficult time making up his work when he returned.

Chris was one of the few people with whom I still spoke, so he informed me of his diagnosis. He told me he had Lyme disease, which is what had caused his wheat allergy. He also told me a few stories about tantrums he had during which he had cussed out his parents and broke everything in sight.

Though this was more than relevant to my situation, I didn't say a word. I knew I didn't have Lyme disease. When the nephrologist had run his tests, I had been tested for Lyme, and the test came back negative. Maybe it was all in my head.

The teachers gave Chris limited accommodations for his makeup work because Catholic schools weren't required by law to give accommodations as public schools were. The teachers were very strict with both of us when it came to making up work.

After his diagnosis, Chris wanted to learn everything he could about the disease. So for a project we had to do, Imagine8, he chose Lyme disease as his topic. Imagine8 was a full-year research project with several smaller class presentations throughout the year. The first of these was due the week after Christmas break.

Chris was the first student to present a project. Until I listened to Chris's presentation, I never really understood what the actual symptoms were and what kind of pain the disease caused. I nearly ignored the entire presentation because it sounded like a reiteration of what Sue had been telling my family for years. I didn't feel it was necessary to listen to the presentation of the rare disease that affected only a small number of people.

After a few weeks, Chris's parents pulled him out of St. Stephan's and sent him to another Catholic school in the area. I thought it was strange that Chris, one of my best friends, would leave all of a sudden, but I was absorbed with my own problems.

I was still feeling awful, and my grades were suffering because of it. Once an honor roll student, I was now struggling to pass. My parents were oblivious to the fact that I was hanging on for dear life in my academic career. Their main concern was finding out what is wrong with me.

I didn't take school seriously, and I tried to waste time in class so I wouldn't have to read, write, or do anything—my mind didn't work, and my hands were nearly crippled. The scary part was when I actually tried, I found my previous abilities weren't there.

We had a reading enhancement program at St. Stephan's for which we would take tests on a computer based on the books we checked out from the library. At the beginning of the year, we took a test to determine our reading level, and each level had a corresponding color code. Every book in the library had a colored sticker on the spine that helped us find books to read at our various levels.

We went to the computer lab to take an online reading test. I read it slowly and stumbled over some words, but thought I'd done okay. During the next class, our teacher gave us each a bookmark. On mine was a green sticker. As a class, we walked to the library to pick out our first books. Other students were comparing stickers; they all had blue or black stickers. I couldn't find anyone else with a green sticker. When we got into the library, our teacher said, "Okay everyone, come up to the desk and check the chart to find out what your reading level is."

I looked at the chart. Black was ninth grade, blue was eighth grade, red was seventh grade, and green was third grade. Karlie, one of my friends, had a purple sticker—tenth grade. Because our library had books only up to the ninth-grade level, she joked that there were no books there for her. Meanwhile, I was in the third-grade section.

I cannot put into words the shame and embarrassment I felt when everyone else in the class was reading a Harry Potter or Twilight book but the highest level I could check out was Goosebumps. I tried to play this off as if I had purposely failed the test so I wouldn't have to read difficult books, but that couldn't have been further from the truth. I made a conscious effort on the preliminary test, but every time I read, the words weren't clear and seemed to be strewn all over the page. I had read at the seventh-grade level the previous year; I was regressing.

My math teacher e-mailed my parents with the news I was failing the class. Though my reading issues were significant, I had more assignments in math than in any other subject—meaning more failed assignments. My parents hired a tutor who came to my house every Monday to review math with me. After the first unit we worked on together, I felt confident I could take the test. After I took it, I felt as if I'd aced it. I was sure of that. When I got it back, my jaw dropped when I saw I'd gotten a 54.

I kept my composure because it was the last period of the day. On my car ride home, I told my dad and started to cry. I got home and went to sleep even though my tutor was coming. My dad came down to my room in the basement to get me when the tutor arrived at three o'clock, and I went berserk. That is one of the few vivid memories I have from that time because it was one of my worst episodes. I screamed and punched a hole in my door. I couldn't handle the fact that I had still failed despite my best efforts.

My father carried me upstairs as I kicked and screamed like a toddler. When we got to the top of the stairs, I screamed at the top of my lungs, "I'm going to kill both of you!" and slammed the door. I can only imagine the amount of terror that caused my tutor, but in about fifteen minutes, my dad calmed me down by letting me have some space. After a few minutes, he said, "Pat, it's okay, I know how hard this has been for you."

"No you don't. No one knows how hard this is for me. I'm done trying," I said.

"Okay, I don't know how you're feeling. I know this is extremely hard for you, but you have to keep moving forward. Just do what you can. It doesn't have to be perfect. Just give it your best effort."

He inspired me to go upstairs and finish the session.

One language arts test was on sentence structure and indirect and direct object pronouns. I made a determined effort to study; my mom and I went over the material for nearly three hours the night before. I took the test the next day and just couldn't remember what direct and indirect objects were. I got a twenty-something on the test. I told my mom that, and she wanted to see the test. I handed it to her.

She looked at it and said, "Oh Patrick, come on, buddy. What are you doing? We went over all this stuff."

"I know, but I just froze and forgot everything."

"What do you mean?"

"The night when we reviewed it, I knew it, but the next day during the test, I didn't remember any of it," I said.

This made her more upset. She raised her voice. "I think you're not trying."

"Mom, I'm doing the best I can!"

"I really don't believe that," she said. She left the room.

Because of how much we had studied the night before, she felt I would have had to have consciously tried to perform as poorly as I had on the test. I received failing grades more often than not, so I wasn't very concerned. After that failed attempt, my parents hired another English teacher at the school to tutor me. I went to his classroom once a week after school to review the material, and with his help, I was able to pass the class.

One day when I went to his classroom for tutoring, he looked at me with a shocked expression. "What happened to your face?" he asked. I had no idea what he was talking about. "Go to the bathroom and look in the mirror," he said.

So I went in, looked in the mirror, and was shocked. Half my face was drooping, and I had no control over it. On the left side of my face, my lip hung halfway down my chin, and I couldn't move it. I had a rash on only the left side of my face. I looked like a strange cross between the phantom from *Phantom of the Opera* and Sloth from *The Goonies*. I was scared.

My parents made me stay home from school for the next few days for fear I was contagious. Within two days, the drooping of my face went away, but the rash remained. Little did I know that this was yet another symptom of Lyme.

"This is getting ridiculous!" I heard my mom yell. "He needs a primary care doctor."

My father made an appointment with another primary care doctor, but he was not accepting new patients. After examining and questioning me, the only thing he could come up with was that the rash was a result of poison oak. The drooping I experienced earlier was a severe rash. He gave me some steroids for that, and after another few days, it cleared up.

Even at home when I tried to escape everything, my body kept me from numbing my pain. Whenever I played video games, my head hurt so badly that I just stared into space. Once, I was playing *Garage Band* alone, and after a few minutes, I went into a hypnotic trance. I remember bits of this experience because it was my first Lyme-induced seizure, but much of this account is what my dad told me later.

The moving colors and flashing lights of the game seemed blinding. I saw a kaleidoscope of color coming from the screen. Blinded by the iridescent glow, I was unable to move. My hands began to tremble and shake. Then my body tensed up entirely as if all of my blood had become cement. I broke out into a cold sweat before my entire body went numb. I began flailing erratically as I fell from the couch to the ground. That episode lasted about two minutes. I was in the basement, and no one heard the commotion. After I regained control, I staggered to my feet. My head was pounding. As I made my way upstairs, each step a challenge, I felt nauseous. I made my way to the kitchen, where my dad was sitting, and I collapsed. I began sobbing, and my dad hurried to my side and asked what had happened.

I yelled over and over, "Make the voices stop!" between sobs.

"What voices?"

"Please, make them stop!" I put my head into my hands and continued weeping.

"Patrick, what's going on?"

Through my sobs, I managed to say, "I was playing video games, and my brain shut off."

He hugged me for what seemed like forever.

I heard voices in my head telling me all my secrets and repressed feelings. Unfortunately, that was the first of many such episodes, and I had to avoid playing video games. That isolated me further from my peers because playing video games was all we did when we got together. We neglected to tell any of the physicians about these episodes because we didn't think they pertained to the rest of my symptoms—plus, what hope was there? The doctors never knew what was wrong; they could never help me.

The entire middle school was required to do a research project called Imagine8; that was the school-year-long project for which my friend Chris had researched Lyme disease. Every student was required to write a research paper, create a presentation board, and give an oral presentation. In the seventh grade, we had to choose a topic that was based on either science or history. I decided to choose a historical figure since I had already done such a successful project in my science class. One of my all-time favorite teachers, Mrs. Paquette, was my history teacher, and I loved history because of her. She was intriguing, funny, and always full of life.

One night while I was collapsed on the couch from exhaustion, I watched one of my favorite shows, *Family Guy*. Peter Griffin, in one of his typical rants of stupidity, was dancing around saying, "Would you like some tea? I would because I'm Winston Churchill." For the next few days, I recited this phrase around the house while doing my best impression, so my mom suggested I do my project on Winston Churchill. I agreed.

As I researched Churchill, I found many of his famous quotes, and these two have stuck with me: "If you're going through hell, keep on going," and "The further back you look, the further forward you will see." These two quotes made perfect sense to me at the time, and they showed me that even during bad times, I could expect good times to come. After I found those quotes, I was intrigued by the man and was excited to do the project—I had a spark of life.

On presentation day, we spoke to judges and the parents of all the students. I dressed up in a full suit and top hat like Winston Churchill. I felt I had wooed the judges with my knowledge. I was very disappointed when I didn't win an award. I was more upset than I should have been. I cried the whole way home, and when I got home, I started screaming and yelling, and I ripped my poster board in half. I blacked out and went into the zone of my typical tantrums. God only knows whom I hit, what I said, and what I broke during that frenzy because my family never spoke of it later. I was fed up with my situation and broke down. What should have been an innocuous letdown turned into rage.

I was devastated because seemingly my best effort hadn't been good enough. I had worked constantly on that project. I had poured every ounce of energy I had into its creation. I'd fought through countless nights of fatigue and mental fog to finish the project on time, but it simply wasn't enough. It was a sickening and deadening feeling to know I had worked ten times harder than everyone else had to complete the same amount of work, yet I was not rewarded for my effort.

Chapter 7
Escalating Outbursts

My life was getting less and less manageable, and I was withdrawing more every day. I didn't really think about it; I guess I just assumed I'd stay alone and in pain until I got better or until I died. I never stopped to consider that I couldn't keep going on the way I was.

One day, I was fooling around with some of my classmates while we waited to be dismissed for the day. I playfully took a book from one of the girls in my class, and kidding around, she lightly punched me in the stomach. Something came over me, and I felt a fire of rage inside. Almost automatically I retaliated. I got into her face, threw the book down, and screamed, "Are you fucking kidding me?" Every ounce of me felt the need to rip her head off. All the rage I had let build up over the year was pounding through my veins and seeping through my pores. It took everything I had not to physically hurt her. I was taught from the time I was young to never hit a girl, and that conditioning took over: I didn't hit her, but my anger permeated my whole being, so instead, I shoved a whole row of desks across the room. My homeroom teacher, Mr. Page, who was in the hallway at the time, came in and sent me to the office of the vice principal, Dr. Conlin.

I broke down on my walk of shame to his office. I was ashamed of what I had done. I had let my emotions get the better of me. I had lost control of who I was as a person. I felt my life was slipping from my fingers, and I was hysterical. In between sobs, I explained the altercation to Dr. Conlin, with whom I had a good relationship. He was shocked and gave me detention. After all the good publicity I had brought to the school from the electric car, it seemed as though I could do whatever

I wanted. Though my behavior had changed drastically, my teachers knew that my mom had cancer. My teachers probably expected my role as a class clown as a defense mechanism, but what I had done was far over the line. Mr. Page didn't hold that incident against me because I'd written in several essays about my mom having cancer. I served the one detention and tried my best to forget about the incident, but it was tattooed on my brain.

Later in the year, I was sitting in Mr. Page's language arts class killing as much time as possible when an Indian girl named Stughti raised her hand and asked a question. I opened my mouth and said loud enough for the whole class could hear, "Stughti Dootie." Stughti started crying, and I and the other twenty immature thirteen-year-olds were laughing away. Mr. Page said I had detention and had to go to the office yet again.

"You're kidding, right?" I asked.

"No. That was totally uncalled for. Go to the office."

I stood up and yelled, "I didn't fucking do anything!"

His face went blank. I looked around and saw expressions of terror on every face in the room. I walked across the room and kicked my backpack into Mr. Page's desk, which propelled the desk two feet forward and left a dent in its metal side. As I made my way toward the door, I heard faint whispers from my frightened classmates. What I picked out most clearly was "What's wrong with him?" I stormed out of the room, slammed the door, and heard it locked behind me.

Once I stepped into the hallway, I knew I had messed up. I was beside myself; I had never acted that way, not since I'd been a kid. Unable to cope with the stress of the situation, I went into the bathroom to cry. The turmoil of my perpetual illness made me prone to outbursts, but I knew I should have been able to keep myself from saying something as vulgar as I had. Mr. Page was one of my favorite teachers, and Stughti was one of my good friends.

I had a knot in my stomach because a nightmare had just come true. I kept replaying the scene in my head and asking myself, *Did you really just do that*? Though I no longer believed in God, I muttered a half-hearted prayer that went something like, "Please help this turn out okay. Don't let Stughti hate me."

I was afraid to go back to class. I thought maybe if I ditched school, everything would be okay. Maybe if I went back to the room, I could pretend as if nothing had happened. I couldn't believe what my life had come to. I wondered if my classmates thought of me as a bigot or an asshole.

Such thoughts rushed through my head as I debated what to do next. I decided if I pretended everything was okay, it would be. I didn't want to go to Dr. Conlin's office for fear of disappointing him further. That would have been my third trip to his office in a month, so I avoided going to his office to preserve my pride and reputation. I wasn't concerned about the punishment; I knew what I had done was wrong. No amount of detentions could have come close to erasing the shame I would have felt by being reprimanded by Dr. Conlin. After my outbursts, I rarely felt remorseful, but Dr. Conlin being disappointed in me was what I feared most. He thought the world of me and had openly told me I was one of his favorite students ever. I wanted to avoid the shame.

I cleaned myself up and went back to Mr. P's room. I realized he wouldn't know whether I'd been to Dr. Conlin's office or not. I tried to open the door, but it was still locked. The feeling of not being able to come back to class transformed my feelings of regret to rage. I felt separated from my peers—an outsider looking in. I wanted to break the barrier, so I smashed my fist once into the door.

I saw Mr. Page through the small glass window. He was livid and noticeably disheveled. He had clearly never experienced actions like mine. He opened the door a crack and spoke to me through it.

"Did Dr. Conlin give you a slip?"

"No. I didn't go. I'll go at the end of the day."

Mr. P looked appalled. "No! Go right now!"

He slammed the door in my face. Once again, I felt cut off from my friends and classmates. I began to tear up. Some of my fears were coming true—the fear of disappointing Dr. Conlin, the fear of being rejected by my classmates, the fear of being hated, and the fear of not being able to control myself.

I walked into Dr. Conlin's office crying. He looked concerned and quickly came around his desk to greet me.

"What's wrong?" he asked with big, soft eyes.

"Mr. Page gave me detention."

"What did you do?"

"I don't know," I said as if I had no idea what had happened twenty minutes prior.

"It's all right. Just calm down. We can wait until the end of the day to speak with him." He gave me a book to read. A few minutes later, he said, "You know, Patrick, I get a lot of kids in here who get detention, and they don't care; it doesn't affect them at all. Because you're so upset, I know you made a mistake and didn't mean to get in trouble. I know you're a good kid." He seemed as though he wanted to protect me; I heard conviction in his voice and saw concern in his eyes. Knowing he was still on my side gave me some reassurance.

After the bell rang, he brought Mr. Page into his office and asked what I had done. He wasn't the same playful teacher I had always known; he was different. He stiffened up, looked at me with daggers in his eyes, and said, "I'd rather not repeat exactly what you said, but you know what you said, and I'll keep that between us unless you'd like to tell him. But what you said is considered bullying, and you deserve a detention."

Dr. Conlin thanked him, and he quickly exited the tiny office.

I was still upset about the whole thing. I was ashamed at having created a problem and wished I could take it back. Yet I didn't feel I'd done anything wrong. I didn't remember doing anything. I had only a foggy memory of what had transpired a few minutes earlier. I remembered sitting in class and then storming out—that's it.

In the days that followed, my classmates seemed to forget about the incident … and they forgot about me even more. My relationship with Mr. Page began to change. He barely spoke to me anymore.

The last week of school was quickly approaching, and on the eighth graders' last day of school, I was giving hugs and saying my good-byes to some of my friends. I had maintained a good relationship with the class ahead of me because those in it hadn't experienced the full effect of my symptoms. I was extremely sad to see them go.

One of my friends, Shanelle, was taking pictures with some of her classmates. Mr. Page saw her as she passed his room. He took her camera and was going to give her detention for use of technology in school, which we all knew wasn't justified. I thought this was ridiculous, and considering she was within hours of graduating, I was frustrated with Mr. Page. I thought of him more of a friend than a teacher, so in that situation, I treated him like a friend. I walked up behind him and slapped him on each side of his face as I'd do when horsing around with my friends. Only later did I understand how wrong that was.

Mr. P was shocked and irate. He screamed, "Get over here!"

The bell had rung to signal the end of the day, so I pretended as if nothing had happened. I walked out the door. In my rush to leave the building so as not to be chased down and reprimanded by Mr. P, I left my backpack in his classroom.

I climbed into my dad's car, and he asked, "How was your day?" I told him it was all right. He turned the car around in the pickup line outside school and parked in the lot. When I asked him what he was doing, he said, "We have to go to Mr. Mongillio and sign the registration for the electric car over to him."

Mr. M's room was connected to Mr. Page's room by a door. "Do you mind if I stay in the car?" I asked.

"Why?"

"I'm really tired. I just want to sleep."

As he exited the car, I asked, "Can you please go to Mr. Page's room and get my backpack? I forgot it there."

My dad was confused, but he said, "Sure."

He was inside for what seemed like an eternity. About half an hour later, he came back with my backpack. "You slapped Mr. Page?"

I was mortified. "It was an accident."

I spent the majority of the car ride home telling him the story. I told him the truth. There was no way to mitigate the situation. I didn't see any benefit to lying and making my situation worse. I overemphasized what I thought Mr. Page had done and how wrong I thought that had been. I painted Mr. P as the villain and myself as the magnificent hero who saved the day. My dad was mad at me but not as mad as I thought he should be. He found it somewhat comical that I'd slapped a teacher because he knew I hadn't done it maliciously. He understood the close relationship I had built with Mr. P over the past few years, and he knew I had simply overstepped my boundaries.

We got home and found ten missed calls and voice mails from the principal, Sr. Renee, saying, "Patrick has in-house suspension and is to report to Dr. Conlin's office first thing tomorrow morning." My parents were disappointed but not mad. They knew what I had been going through. Still, the next day, I pretended as if nothing had happened and went to my normal classes. By second period, I thought I was home free and wouldn't have to serve the suspension. But halfway through my science class with Mr. Mongillio, Sr. Renee, Dr. Conlin, and Mr. Page walked into the classroom and asked if they could see me. My heart dropped because I knew what was coming. My worst nightmare was coming true. I had no one on my side, and the two most powerful people in the school were out to get me.

I stepped into the hallway to speak with them. Sr. Renee said, "We told you on the phone to stop in to see Dr. Conlin first thing to serve your suspension. What you did to Mr. Page was wildly inappropriate, and you will be serving in-house suspension for the last week of the school year."

I regretted what I had done, but I was more ashamed of their perception of the changed me than of the actual punishment. I went back to my classroom to get my books and then went to Dr. Conlin's office.

Since it was the last week of school, I had no work to do, so the majority of the time I sat and stared at the wall. I was more bored than anything, but the thought that they were going to hate me kept slipping into my mind. That was my biggest fear.

Sr. Renee, Dr. Conlin, and Mr. Page had always viewed me as an exemplary student and the face of everything St. Stephan's stood for, but that had changed. Even Dr. Conlin, who loved me and would always talk to me, didn't say a word to me the entire week. The only connection we made was occasional, awkward eye contact, and he always looked disappointed.

I sat there and considered my life. I wondered why my fingers hurt so much and why my joints were so swollen. I wondered why all this was happening to me. I thought that just a few months before, I had been at the top of the world, but at that point, I felt I was at the bottom. The only contact I had with my peers that week was when I went to the cafeteria to get lunch. Dr. Conlin escorted me to ensure I didn't talk to anyone.

His eyes were fixed on me. The cafeteria went nearly silent as if I were a circus animal brought to the trough for feeding. Vacant stares and muffled whispers took the place of normal lunchtime chatter. I felt I was an outsider and no longer belonged there. I had become the antithesis of who I used to be. It felt as if everyone was looking down on me and talking about me behind my back.

Everything I had was slipping away. I tried desperately to cling on to what I still had, but I soon realized that was out of my control. My relationships with everyone around me had changed in some way or another. Dr. Conlin had always been one of my biggest fans, but at that point, I was just … nothing. I was fading away. I lost a little more of myself with every angst- and pain-filled moment. I wasn't who I had always been.

That was the first time I stared into my eyes in the mirror and asked, *Who am I?*

Chapter 8

I'm Going to Sleep All Summer

I served my weeklong suspension and missed out on our annual field day. I was relieved that the stressful year was finally over.

When my dad picked me up the last day of school, the first thing I said to him was, "I'm going to sleep all summer." Without waiting for a response, I fell asleep. When we got home, I slept on the couch for hours. I remember that day clearly because of the extreme rainstorms outside that mimicked my inner storms.

My baseball season had just finished. I had no plans whatsoever. I had stopped talking to my friends from school months before, so I spent the first few weeks of summer sleeping. I hardly ever got out of bed. When I did, I moved only from my bed to the couch and back again. When I sat up, an excruciating pain shot up my back. Usually, it would lock out and I would fall back to wherever I was lying. My joints were still like an unlubricated tin man's. All the energy drained from my body along with all motivation to do anything. I didn't see daylight for three weeks. My only aspiration was to sleep. I was tired to the extent that I dreamed about sleeping. My eyelids seemed glued shut. Even while I slept, I heard bits of conversations from my family members. My sisters would ask, "He's still sleeping?" with disgust in their voices, and my parents argued over my illness.

"Maybe this is all in his head," my mom finally admitted.

"You don't see him struggle everyday as much as I do. There's something wrong, and we're going to figure out what it is," my dad insisted.

I'd been ill for more than a year, and my mother was fed up. She started to believe I was depressed and my symptoms were psychosomatic. My dad knew I was sick as he had spent the most time with me. I was the cause of many heated debates and sleepless nights in my house, but I was unconscious in my bedroom. "Patrick, it's time to wake up" became background noise—even I knew it was no use.

Time passed, and days blended; sleeping twenty-six hours at a time will have that effect on a person. I was alone in the biggest fight of my life. Toward the end of the school year, I had become reclusive, but during that summer, I became almost mute. I communicated through grunts while I was half-asleep or through yelling during my belligerent tantrums. I was nearly unable to move. I ate all my meals in bed. The only times I left my bed or the couch were when I staggered to the bathroom, each step more painful than the last. The stiffness that had previously affected my hands and knees made its way to my neck and back. Excruciating pain surged through my body every time I moved or turned my head.

I had very bad night sweats. I felt I'd just gotten out of the shower every time I woke up. It was summer, but the temperature didn't account for every inch of my sheets being drenched in sweat. Due to this new symptom, I was referred to an infectious disease doctor. He said the only thing that induced night sweats was HIV/AIDS. Since I was thirteen and had never had a blood transfusion or sex, I thought that was highly unlikely. After he ordered a series of tests and they all came back negative, the doctor thought I might have mononucleosis. He ran an Epstein-Barr test, and it came back positive. My parents and I were relieved because we knew we were finally getting somewhere. This finally gave us some hope, but not much.

Mono accounted for the fatigue and achiness but not the arthritis, tantrums, brain issues, or night sweats. I became somewhat optimistic based on this new diagnosis, but I knew it didn't tell the whole story. It was a glimmer of hope, but I'd been suffering for well over a year with no answers. Even that diagnosis couldn't bring me back from the point of wanting to give up.

My family is Roman Catholic; we went to church every Sunday, but I never saw the purpose of going. That summer, I saw even less reason to go to church than I had before, so every Sunday, I intentionally slept past five in the afternoon so I didn't have to go to Mass. My rejection of God became so strong that I removed everything that stood for religion from my room. Pictures, quotes, and rosary beads were ripped to shreds, and I even set my Bible on fire. I felt betrayed by God; I thought He had done this to me.

Though I had never felt like I got a lot out of going to church, I practiced religion in my own way. Prior to my illness, I read verses from the Bible whenever I was struggling with a problem, and I prayed almost every night. But once I got sick, I became frustrated with my situation as a whole and began to lash out. I no longer wanted physical reminders of the God who had left me. I was malevolent. I began listening to heavy metal music. Anything with as much screaming as possible mirrored my internalized frustration and anger. I often felt tears trickling down my face when I was semiconscious. I had no outlet to express my feelings of worthlessness because I spent most of my days sleeping. I had no motivation to live.

I was still able to speak, but I had nothing to say, no desire to communicate with anyone. That was the worst symptom I'd suffered. I had lost my identity, and I had forgotten who I was. The lively, passionate, energetic kid who I used to be was gone. I had no real idea of who I was. Sleeping for well over twenty hours a day caused a loss of communication with my family. I had no reason to speak, so I chose not to. It seemed like the only time I talked was when I screamed during one of my tantrums. Every day when I woke up at five or six at night, I was frustrated at not only myself but also everyone around me. I was disappointed in myself for sleeping the day away. Every time I woke up in the midafternoon or early evening, one of my family members gave me a very sarcastic "Good morning." I hated my family for believing that sleeping that much was my choice.

"Shut up! Honestly, you don't know what I'm going through," I said one time to that remark.

"How hard is it to wake up, seriously?" one of my sisters asked. That was my tipping point. I screamed, yelled, threw things, hit my family members, punched holes in walls, and ran outside to express my frustration. My sisters' and parents' arms were covered in bruises from our altercations.

Such tantrums began happening more often than not—about every other day. The simplest things set me off. If there was a sudden change of plans or if something didn't go the way I wanted, I went ballistic.

Three months prior, while I was still barely able to function, one of my worst tantrums had transpired. My baseball team was playing in an out-of-town tournament, and my family was staying in a hotel for the night. After one of the games, my parents asked my sisters and me, "Where do you guys want to go for dinner?" We agreed on a Chinese place across the street from our hotel. After driving the ten minutes to the restaurant, Mikaela said, "I don't feel really good. Can we go somewhere else?" Alicia chimed in, "Yeah. This place doesn't look too great."

My mom said, "There's a bunch of restaurants down the street. Why don't we keep driving?"

I yelled, "No! We said we were going here, so that's what we're going to do!"

I had an absolute meltdown. Rage coursed through my body. I was sitting in the backseat on the driver's side. I violently punched the window with the side of my fist—I needed to get out of there—I shoved the door open to free myself and ran around the parking lot. I began to yell to show the world my frustration. My parents tried to corral me, but I was determined to escape. As my parents inched closer and closer, I yelled, "Leave me alone!" My parents finally grabbed me and brought me back to the hotel room. Along the way, they tried to calm me. "It's going to be okay. Just take some deep breaths."

Back in the room, I locked myself in the bathroom still crying and yelling. My parents picked the lock with a coat hanger and tried to calm me down, but their soft voices were no longer working. I began banging on the walls and throwing things. I screamed whatever came into my head: "Why am I here? I don't like you! I want to take you and throw you. I'm going to light you on fire. I will fucking kill you." I didn't realize I made no sense. I had no filter.

"I will kill you" seemed to be my new favorite phrase. I felt the need to inflict the pain I was feeling on others. I was hurting, so I wanted them to hurt. I wanted them to understand what I was going through.

As I continued to scream and carry on, still wearing my baseball uniform, my parents turned the shower on and drenched me. This calmed me instantly. I gently began crying and hyperventilating. When I finally composed myself, I looked across the bathroom into the foggy mirror. I stared at myself and wondered why I had acted that way. I saw a distorted image of myself that couldn't be wiped away. I continued to cry and kept asking myself *Why?* and *Who am I?* I knew these actions were not just out of character; they were also beyond my control.

Episodes like that happened throughout the summer as well; I continued to ask the question *Who am I?* After over four months of the cycle of sleeping in, throwing a tantrum, and sleeping again, I realized that something needed to change, that I had to do something with my life. It was July, and during a rare moment while I was both awake and calm, I said, "I don't want to live this way anymore."

I questioned how much longer that this pain would last. I knew that though it felt like it at the time, my situation wouldn't be like that forever. I needed to give life another try. I realized I could reinvent myself. I needed to break the cycle. I found that I was the only one with the power to change my situation. I found a reason to wake up, a reason to keep pushing forward, a reason to live.

I wanted to play hockey again. I knew in my heart that I wasn't giving life all I had. I knew there was more inside of me no matter how tired I was.

After my severe concussion, my primary care doctor had told me I could never play contact sports again, but he had retired, so I decided I was cleared to play. My parents thought it was a great idea because it would give me a positive outlet for all my aggression and give me something to look forward to.

That summer, I bought hockey equipment and a net to practice shooting at home. At first, I practiced with tennis balls, but even that was strenuous at times. My swollen fingers were hardly able to grasp the wooden stick, but still I tried.

By the end of July, I was able to stay awake for six hours a day, usually from 3:00 to 9:00 p.m. I spent every moment possible in my driveway shooting hundreds of times into the net. The first steps in the morning were the most challenging as was the first shot. But once my blood started flowing, my back didn't ache for the time being and I was achy but functional.

My frustration drove me beyond my physical symptoms. Instead of keeping my frustration bottled up, I decided to use it to push me. Each time I shot into the net, I let out a grunt, a battle cry of sorts; I was going to fight. I taught myself to skate by going every day to the rink. My pride took backseat. I was willing to fall and look stupid to reach my goal. Eventually, when I got my feet under me, I would play public hockey in the afternoon. Hockey gave me a purpose, something to look forward to, something to work at and improve on. I still had trouble getting out of bed for it, but I was determined. My sisters noted my efforts and encouraged me to get up and play even during my worst days.

I had no friends at the time, and I would constantly ask myself, *Who would miss me if I died? No one would even notice.* I finally knew what I needed. If I didn't wake up for hockey, I'd have no purpose, no reason to get out of bed or even to live. Hockey gave me the opportunity to feel alive again.

The first day at public hockey, which consisted of a half-hearted scrimmage between players of all ages and skill levels, I fit right in even though I was pretty bad. But after I began playing, I noticed something very unusual. After about two minutes of light skating, I was sweating profusely but I wasn't out of breath. By the end of the two hours of playing, I felt like I weighed three hundred pounds because my pads had absorbed all my sweat. I went back to the locker room, changed out of the drenched equipment, lay on the bench, and fell asleep. A phone call from my dad woke me up about half an hour later. But I felt a different kind of exhaustion. That physical exertion left me with a feeling of accomplishment rather than worthlessness. I was tired because I had lived. I was tried because I was fighting for my life—not to save it but to live it.

Chapter 9
The Diagnosis

I was coming out of my hibernation, coming back to myself, but that didn't fix everything. I was still sick and lonely, and as I began to think more about what was happening and who I wanted to be, there were more and more questions. What was my illness? What did it mean about who I was? My illness didn't define me, but I was still searching for what it was.

We didn't know what was wrong with me, but I felt emotional and physical pain, and I never got so much as one phone call or text message asking how I was doing. Everyone thought I was either lazy for sleeping all day or insane because of my many outbursts. I felt I didn't exist to most people.

A little boy who lived in my city had Osteosarcoma. When the residents of the city found out he had cancer, they held fundraisers to help pay for his chemotherapy and traveling costs for him and his family to and from Boston. No matter where I went, I saw slogans plastered on billboards or bumper stickers, for him. It seemed that everyone was rooting for him to make a recovery.

That made me feel bad about my own illness … and about myself. Everyone knew what was wrong with him, and he was treated as some kind of hero, accepting awards. Balloons and flowers were brought to his house every time he came back from a chemo treatment. Each time we passed by their house, I wondered, *why couldn't I have had cancer or some other kind of disease that people actually knew about?* I grew resentful toward a boy I didn't even know. Everyone was there for him— but I was alone. Though I wanted to be myself again, I was envious.

I started to doubt myself. I'd always been so sure I was sick, but I started asking myself, *Am I really?* I thought back to when my mom was first diagnosed with breast cancer. Nearly every day, someone brought food, flowers, or supportive cards. Our house was overflowing with sympathetic gifts. That made me bitter. My mom's illness was easy to understand, and it was part of the reason we hadn't yet found out what was wrong with me—her illness had overshadowed mine. It made sense to me on the surface, but there I was, still sick.

Discovering that my mom was battling cancer also contributed to the myriad diagnoses of my symptoms as psychosomatic. The medical professionals I saw at the time felt I was dealing with depression from seeing my mother in that condition and was crying out for attention. At that point, months after her diagnosis and the start of my illness, that was starting to make sense to me. I began to doubt the conviction I'd had for so long. Maybe I had been embellishing my symptoms as a subconscious plea for attention from those around me. Perhaps I slept all the time to avoid the fear of having a parent battle a potentially terminal illness. But one fact kept me from fully doubting my sanity: after a year of chemotherapy and radiation, my mom made a full recovery and entered remission, and yet my symptoms persisted.

What's wrong with me? The question I'd pushed away while I slept was back. Though playing hockey alleviated some of my pain, I was still suffering and sleeping twenty hours a day with little to no improvement.

We seemed to be out of options. My dad frequently spoke with Sue about my situation. Throughout all of my suffering, she still insisted I had Lyme disease. When the nephrologist ran the litany of tests, he made sure to test for Lyme disease. But like all the others, the test had come back negative. I didn't have Lyme; we had proof of that, but Sue still insisted I did. She said there was one form of Lyme that attacks the sinuses and would account for all of my symptoms: pain, lethargy, night sweats—everything.

Why did no one think of this sooner?

"The standard blood test for Lyme tests for only one strain and often comes back a false negative," Sue explained.

We were skeptical about that. Why hadn't any of the doctors

suggested it? We did some research on our own. The data we found proved that even if I did have Lyme, it usually lasted only for a month or two, which wouldn't have accounted for my nearly two years of suffering. The Massachusetts General Hospital website[3] had almost no information about Lyme disease; it was as if it didn't exist. Sue disagreed. She believed that chronic Lyme disease did exist because she had been battling it herself for ten years. She was convinced I had Lyme, but my mom and dad were not very interested in this idea because my parents questioned the validity of my cousin's practice. "She thinks everyone has Lyme," they often said.

After much family discussion, we decided we would pay Sue a visit—we were skeptical but desperate. We were skeptical because we refused to believe that all of my suffering—the years of arthritic symptoms, continuous congestion, brain fog, physical deterioration, and furious anger—all had a single cause, Lyme disease. But my parents believed that perhaps it could be the cause of some if not all my symptoms. Sue said I should have blood drawn and send it to a lab in California called IGeneX for a unique test.

"This is a very expensive blood test," she said, "but they're the only lab in the country that will test the blood carefully enough to find the different strains of Lyme in the blood." We were running out of options, so my parents decided to make the steep investment.

We had to wait about six weeks for the results, during which time I continued to get worse. I stopped playing hockey because I no longer had the energy and because my body hurt so much.

The stress wore on our family. During my twenty- to thirty-hour hibernations, I could hear my parents arguing about me, and my stomach was in knots. They would argue that the "experimental" Lyme blood tests were not worth the money, and my mom would always say, "We need to take him to a *real* doctor." My dad would get enraged and say, "All the 'real' doctors don't know what's wrong with him, so isn't this worth a shot?" These arguments grew louder and more passionate as the days wore on. Our family was being torn apart, and I felt responsible—my health determined what we did as a family.

Once that summer, family members visited from Ohio, and we went to Newport, Rhode Island, for a weekend. On the first night we were at the hotel, we agreed that we wanted to go to the beach the next day. I decided to go to sleep at nine o'clock so I'd be ready. I wanted to go; I didn't want to hold everyone back. But I woke up feeling worse than when I'd gone to sleep. I looked at the clock, which read 2:30 p.m. Apparently, every member of my family—including my cousins—had tried to wake me up with no luck. I felt I'd let my family down.

My family and extended family members had waited for me. We finally arrived at the beach at 3:00 p.m. Even though it was 85 degrees when we got to the beach, I was freezing, and I was in a sweat suit. I barely made it to the spot where everyone was putting stuff down before I collapsed in the warm sand and fell asleep. After what felt like just a few minutes, my parents woke me up and said it was time to go—it had been nearly three hours.

The summer came to an end. I faced eighth grade. The prospect was daunting. I knew I wasn't ready physically or mentally to combat the daily grind of school. I thought that going back to school would mean setting myself up for disaster.

While he was driving me to my first day of eighth grade, my dad said, "We got the results back from the blood test."

"So do I have Lyme?" I asked quietly.

"Yes," my dad answered, "but not just Lyme disease. You also have Bartonella and Babesia[4]—two co-infections."

I knew what the effects of Lyme were, but I had never heard of the other two things. *How is that possible?*

My dad continued, "The fatigue, headaches, and night sweats are from the Babesia. The swollen glands and sinuses and the seizures are from the Bartonella, and the outbursts and joint aches are from the Lyme."

The moment that the thought *But I was never bitten by a tick* came into my head, it all came back to me. *The blood. The shower. The tick.* "Do you remember a few weeks after Camp Crescent Moon when I said I had a tick on the back of my head?"

My dad gestured openly with his hands off the steering wheel as if to say, *How could I possibly remember that?* He looked briefly at the ceiling of the car as if it held the answer. He thought for a moment and gave me an almost confused "No."

"Come on!" I implored. "That day after school when I came out of the shower and told you I had a tick on the back of my head."

He remained silent.

I was becoming frustrated. "You have to remember that." I crossed my arms and stared at the floor. *How could I have been so stupid?*

"This was right after Camp Crescent Moon?"

"Maybe two weeks after," I said.

He looked away from the road briefly to make eye contact.

"You said it was only tangled in your hair."

"I lied to you," I said. My dad looked confused. "I didn't think it was a big deal."

"Patrick, why would you do that?"

"I didn't think the tick had been on me for that long." I never put it together that it was from Camp Crescent Moon. I knew the tick was lodged in my skin, but my former self reasoned that perhaps it was from my yard or a baseball field.

"It's okay," he said softly. "It can be treated, but it won't be easy."

I felt crushed. I was more angry at myself for being too proud to tell my father that the tick had bitten me than I was upset by my impending treatment. But our conversation didn't inspire a tantrum. I felt devastated. I believed I'd done this to myself. It seemed so clear all of a sudden. *Yet how can this be?* I'd been to doctor after doctor; I'd been tested for Lyme, though only one strain. How had we not figured this out sooner? How had I suffered so much from the bite of one tiny insect?

I suddenly realized that one bite had changed my life. The tick I had extracted from my skull nearly two years prior—an event, like the tick itself, that had seemed so innocuous at the time—had been the beginning of my suffering. That one insect made me doubt my life and myself in general. Lyme disease had changed who I was as a person and drained me of my energy and my motivation to live. Every aspect of my life had been altered because of that one bite simply because I hadn't listened to the camp counselors' cautions.

This insight was a lot to process. I made connections in my brain, almost justifying my actions over the course of the last few years. It finally made sense why I had no control over my body and I felt as if

I'd been brainwashed. Lyme disease infected my brain and spinal cord, which effectively hindered my central nervous system.

Sue insisted I start on a course of antibiotics immediately. She informed us that for every month of undiagnosed Lyme, two months of antibiotics were required. I had gone undiagnosed for eighteen months. My brain capacity was diminished, but I knew my journey had just been extended three more years.

My parents were more than relieved. The period of ambiguity was over. They finally felt able to support their sick child. The diagnosis also came with a spark of hope: what was wrong with me could be fixed. I was shocked. I had already suffered for so long, yet learning my diagnosis was only the beginning. It was bittersweet. I thought it would be a quick fix—I'd read that Lyme could be treated in thirty days. But again, my life wasn't that simple. Sue reassured me that I could in fact be cured, but knowing I had to keep fighting was frustrating. In fact, I needed to fight harder than I ever had in my life. Getting my diagnosis ended up discouraging me, but at least I could tell people what was wrong with me. The illness was no longer all in my head, and it finally had a name.

Chapter 10
Recovery Is Not Soon Enough

I began eighth grade with a diagnosis. I could finally give my symptoms a name. I could finally tell people I wasn't just a lazy teenager with sudden outbursts, body aches, and sinus infections. I wanted everyone to know why I had been sick for the last two years. I wanted to tell them that I was still myself underneath. Though I had a name for my sickness, it still carried a stigma.

I walked through the doors on that first day believing it was the start of the year I'd finally feel like myself again. I walked alone into the empty gymnasium, my sneakers squeaking on the floor. I was early to school for the first time in years. I waited anxiously on the wobbly wooden bleachers as my classmates soon filed in. Jarred sat next to me.

"Hey man! How've you been?" he asked.

"I mean … I'm okay." I was still thinking about my diagnosis.

"What's going on?"

"I'm still sick."

"Still?" He was shocked. "Don't they know what's wrong with you?"

I chuckled. "Actually, they do. I had a blood test a few weeks back, and my dad just told me the results."

"Okay." His eyes opened wider because he knew there was hope.

"I have Lyme disease."

"Oh thank God it's not serious! Wait, but—" he considered what I had just told him. "You've been sick for a while."

"I know. That's the problem."

"Doesn't Lyme only last for a month or two?" he asked.

"Yeah, that's the problem."

I was interrupted by the voice of Sr. Renee obviously speaking too closely to the microphone. "Everyone please take your seats. Kids, please settle down." The students paid little attention.

When Dr. Conlin grabbed the microphone and said, "Excuse me!" we became instantly silent.

Sr. Renee gently took the mic back from Dr. Conlin and uttered a quiet, "Thank you. Welcome, everyone, to the new school year. I'm very excited about this year. But before we begin, let's say the 'Suscipe.'"

We all dreaded that moment. Every time we met as a school, we sang the "Suscipe," a prayer about Catherine McCauley, the founding nun of the Sisters of Mercy. They had founded St. Stephan's School to educate poor and sick children. The eighth graders in particular disliked the song because they learned it not by choice but by constant repetition.

After the prayer, Dr. Conlin told the eighth graders that this year was not a blow-off year by any means: our grades determined which high school we'd go to. "Don't make eighth grade the best two years of your life," he said.

But I knew I'd coast through my final year at St. Stephan's I was done suffering. My focus was on feeling like myself again before going to high school. Though I was determined to recover, most of my classmates didn't support me or understand what was happening to me. I wanted to make eighth grade different, but my symptoms persisted. I went to the first two days of school before becoming too exhausted to function. I missed Wednesday, Thursday, and Friday of that first week.

When I returned to school on Monday, I was greeted with hostility. I found my seat in homeroom next to my friend Peter; my friend Hayden was in front of me. Peter turned to me and asked, "How was your long weekend?"

I felt he was being sarcastic, but I knew he was just asking.

"It was okay," I muttered.

"Did you go anywhere fun?"

"No," I said knowing what was coming.

"Then what were you doing?"

"I was sick."

"Geez, it must have been pretty bad."

"Yeah, it was."

Hayden, overhearing the conversation, whipped around. "What was it?"

"I have Lyme disease."

"Oh yeah, my dog has that," Peter said.

"Lyme disease?" Hayden asked. "How'd you get that?"

"I was bit by a tick."

"Is it bad?"

I nodded. "Yeah," was all I said. I couldn't begin to explain how bad it was.

"What are the symptoms?" Peter asked.

"It makes me extremely tired. I sleep sixteen or eighteen hours a day. My body hurts nonstop, and I feel horrible all the time."

They chuckled. "Welcome to being a teenager," Hayden said.

I wanted to cry. My classmates were invalidating my symptoms just as my doctors had. I realized I had to get through the year and go on to high school. I figured that I could be reclusive and find myself once I was healthy. I knew that a year from that point, regardless of how I was feeling, I'd be going to Bishop Feehan High, an elite, private school. Some said that getting accepted was all about whom you knew. My family's legacy would get me through the doors. Most of my family had gone there, and my mom in particular had a great reputation at the school. She had been a stellar student, athlete, and class president; she was considered one of the most exemplary students to ever graduate from Bishop Feehan. I thought that no matter what I did in eighth grade, I'd be accepted. I believed eighth grade would be a blow-off year. I projected myself into the future, beyond eighth grade, beyond my illness, into my life as a healthy high school student; that was what drove me forward.

I still wasn't well. I hadn't begun a course of treatment, so I was still absent between three and four days a week and my temper was still explosive. I managed to get into a fight with one of my teachers by the second week of school.

We had a new English teacher. She had just graduated from college and had e-mailed all the students about our reading assignment for the summer: *The King's Fifth,* a novel about the Spanish embargoes, and *Alabama Moon,* a story about a boy and his adventures when he ran away from home. My parents bought me the books, but I had had no intention of reading them, so I'd tossed them into a corner of my room. A week before school started, my dad saw the books still in the bag and sarcastically asked, "How are the books coming?"

I simply replied, "I'm not reading them."

"Why?"

"Because reading makes my head hurt."

After I attempted to read the first page of *Alabama Moon* aloud, stuttering and losing my place constantly, my dad asked, "Why don't I read the next page, and we can switch off?" After my dad read the next page, I picked it up again. Each page took me nearly ten minutes to read aloud. After about half an hour, my dad took over all the reading without saying anything. I rested my head on the pillow and listened.

After several days, my dad finished reading the book to me. For my assignment, I had to draw a picture and answer some questions. The final product of the drawing looked as if it had been done by a kindergartener. Scribbled sketches and stray colored pencil marks covered the white piece of paper.

Two days before school started, I still had the entire other book to read. My father and I skimmed *The King's Fifth* together. The assignment for this book was to create a book cover that depicted the main characters in a drawing on the front and a summary of the book on the inside flap. I didn't remember one thing from that book because we had barely read it. My dad trusted I would actually write the essay rather than plagiarizing it or turning in nothing at all.

My hands were too crippled to write by hand, but I was still able to type on the computer. I didn't remember anything from skimming the book, and I didn't care, so I copied and pasted a summary from the Internet, then retyped some of it in my own words. It felt good to have completed the project even if I'd cheated. I was tired of being a failure, so my conscience went out the window.

About three days later, my new teacher called me out into the hallway and quietly shut the door behind her. She took off her glasses. "We need to talk about your summary of *The King's Fifth*."

"What about it?"

"You plagiarized it. There's no way you wrote that; it's way above your writing level."

I got angry. I looked at my four-and-a-half-foot teacher and yelled, "I'm not fucking retarded! I know how to write a damn summary!"

Her jaw dropped. "Go to Dr. Conlin's office. You have a detention for that, and you're waiting on another one for plagiarizing."

It was starting already. I walked in, and Dr. Conlin was happy to see me. He asked how my summer was and why I was there. I replied, "Ms. Hamilton accused me of plagiarizing."

"Well, we have software that can tell us if something's plagiarized or not."

I knew I was screwed. Even though I had put some of the summary in my own words, there were some key phrases I'd let stand word for word. No one would know the result until Dr. Conlin got the papers from my teacher, but once again, I found myself crying in Dr. Conlin's office.

"This is a bad start to the year," he said, "so I'll defend you on this one. Try to get off on the right foot. Don't make eighth grade the best two years of your life."

I never admitted to plagiarizing. Dr. Conlin was once my English teacher. He knew that English was my favorite class and was sure I'd never plagiarize.

I stayed in his office for the remainder of the class period to avoid my new teacher. She sent an e-mail home to my parents explaining that I was accused of plagiarizing. Luckily, her e-mail didn't include what I had said to her, and she hadn't written it on the detention slip for Dr. Conlin either. My parents were a little shocked by the e-mail and asked if I had cheated. I lied.

The next day, my teacher called me into the hallway again. She also brought Peter. My heart was racing. She said calmly to the both of us, "I put both of your summaries into the plagiarism software." She looked at me and said, "I am so sorry. I'm sorry if I offended you yesterday. I should have gotten to know you better before I said that." I was shocked.

She turned to Peter. "You, on the other hand, are a different story. Every word of your summary was plagiarized."

Later that day, I found out he had actually read the book and written a summary all by himself. The young teacher must have mixed the two of us up in person because she didn't know our names. By nothing short of a miracle, I had escaped the situation totally unscathed after not only deliberately plagiarizing but also after cussing out a teacher. Not only that, she had apologized to me. While I should have felt guilty about Peter getting in trouble instead of me, all I could think was, *Oh yeah, my dog has that.* Finally, it seemed that luck was on my side.

While I didn't care about my classes, I wanted to make the best of the year by getting involved in as many things as possible to rebuild my tainted reputation and keep myself moving to avoid excessive sleep. I ran for student council secretary. I made posters, stickers, buttons, and pins with my slogan, "Don't be fat, wear a hat, stroke your cat, and vote for Pat." This showed my classmates I was starting to become the old outgoing, fun me again. I gave a speech in front of the entire middle school. I wrote it with my mom and incorporated all the reasons why I would be the best candidate. And I won.

My life was still very much the same—I was tired, angry, missing school, failing—when I finally began treatment for Lyme disease. I was prescribed my first regimen of antibiotics, which consisted of doxycycline, minocycline, and erythromycin. Sue prescribed these antibiotics. I was extremely lucky because she was one of the only practicing Lyme professionals within 200 miles. Other doctors would have given me a month of doxycycline and pronounce me cured, but that wouldn't have worked for the two co-infections.

I thought getting treated would be the first step toward recovery, but the antibiotics made me even more tired and angry, and they exacerbated all my symptoms. I was sleeping even more than before, and my tantrums were continuing. No one at St. Stephan's directly said anything to me regarding my illness except for the nurse. She said I was welcome to come to her office any time I wasn't feeling well. I felt like I had a free pass because of the publicity the electric car project had brought to the school. No one ever said anything to me about my absences, but my teachers, similar to years past, were frustrated. I was hardly ever in school, and when I was, I was either zoned out or provoking my class into uproars of laughter.

I was determined to spend the year recovering from my illness, which required a significant amount of sleep. I felt it was more important to rest my mind and body than to expend my energy on schoolwork. I received some snide remarks from my teachers, but I was never punished for not turning in my work for the first few weeks of school.

But after the first few weeks, I was sinking in my math class. We had had three quizzes and two tests, and I had failed them all. One Monday, I walked up to my math teacher's desk. He showed me a pile of papers and said, "You should try these again."

He went over each of the tests and quizzes with me.

"Fifty-six ... Fifty-six ... Fifty-six ... Fifty-six ... Fifty-six," he said. "At least you're consistent." I felt he was laughing at me.

After the first month of school, I took an extended leave of absence. I missed all October and the first week of November. During that time, I ate almost nothing and lost over twenty-five pounds. I suffered from my worsening symptoms, and after six weeks on antibiotics, my lethargy got even worse. My symptoms were exacerbated because I suffered from the Herxheimer reaction—a reaction to the bacteria killed by the antibiotics; the bacteria release toxins that cause inflammation.[5] My already swollen joints became immovable, and my sinuses became even more irritated. I spent most days lying on the couch with a warm towel over my face. My parents had pity on me. Every day, they checked on me and spent some time with me. I was usually sleeping, but I could still sense them sitting near me. The process was crushing me. I began to realize it would be an extended battle.

When I returned to school in November, my classmates greeted me with open arms. At first, they accepted me because it was the first time they'd seen me in weeks. I was peppered with questions: "Where were you?" "What were you doing?" "We thought you wouldn't come back." "The teachers were talking about you."

That struck a nerve. I felt helpless while in bed; I realized people had been judging me while I was away. I had no reply to their questions or statements. The brutal truth was that I had spent nearly two months in bed.

Physically, I felt weak. I was hardly able to climb up to the third floor of the school building. I was excited to be back, but I realized what I had missed; I was greeted with a mountain of makeup work. I was as buried in work as I was with questions about where I had been. I was expected to comprehend six weeks of academic material as soon as possible, an arduous task even with an able body and a fully functioning brain. Overwhelmed, I decided the best course of action was to do nothing.

On top of the pile of papers from all my six subjects was a blue sign-up form for basketball. I'd played basketball at St. Stephan's since fourth grade. The coach and I didn't get along—we were both very passionate and opinionated individuals, and I always seemed to find myself yelling at him. Content not to play basketball, I ripped up the paper and threw it in the trash. Playing basketball or doing anything other than recovering seemed trivial and counterproductive at that point. Even if I had been healthy, I didn't want any part of my tyrannical coach or basketball ever again.

Our class had seventeen students, but only six were boys. The five boys minus me made up our basketball team. I attended the first game and sat in the stands to taunt my coach. Every player was forced to play every second of the game. I nearly felt the excruciating pain they must have felt. I watched their sweat drip to the hardwood. I felt sorry for my classmates, but to me, playing basketball was not worth the emotional and physical pain. Then, one of the players took a hard fall under the basket and was injured. They finished the game with four players. I saw how exhausted my classmates were, and I felt bad for them. However, I didn't feel guilty for not playing; I was experiencing enough pain as it was.

A few days later, my dad said, "Your coach called me."

I was puzzled.

"He said if you don't play for the team this year, they'll have to forfeit the team for the eighth-grade season because they couldn't play with just four players. Your coach said he was willing to make a peace agreement and promised he wouldn't yell at you."

I was furious. I believed the coach's promise was nothing more than a simple plea to get me to play.

"If you play this year, I'll give you $500 and these tickets to a Red Sox–Yankee game next week," my dad said.

I didn't know why my father wanted me to play so badly. He hated my coach nearly as much as I did. Perhaps he thought that playing a sport again might distract me from my situation. But his offer was too good to pass up. I accepted it.

I began to play, but I wasn't happy about it. I was still battling symptoms, still barely making it to school, still failing, still not caring. One day, I didn't go to school because I woke up at two in the afternoon. However, I knew there would be an eighth-grade scrimmage between the boys' and girls' teams at the end of the day, and I wanted to participate. I knew that would be a way of making amends with some of my classmates, a way for them to see I was on my way to recovery. I convinced my parents to take me to school for the game.

I snuck through the backdoor of the gym and joined my teammates on the bench. When my name was called for introductions, I jumped up from the bench, and the crowd gave me a standing ovation—everyone in the school knew me as the kid who'd built the electric car, as the student council secretary, or as the class clown who hit a teacher.

I was lined up for the tip-off when Sr. Renee marched onto the court and said, "You did not come to school today. You cannot play." As I walked to the bench, the crowd booed and jeered. I gave the crowd an appreciative wave. That was invigorating. The entire student body was behind me, as we all had one common enemy.

The girls' team lent us a player so we could play. I watched the game from the bench.

After the game ended, Sr. Renee came up to my father and me.

"Why did you not go to school today?"

"Because he was sick," my dad replied.

Sr. Renee looked at him with disgust. "Well, judging by the way he jumped off the bench and was ready to play, he seems fine to me."

"If school started at two in the afternoon, he'd be fine," my dad said, "but the Lyme disease makes him so tired he cannot get out of bed."

Sr. Renee seemed disappointed. She walked away without responding.

I arrived at the next game exhausted and angry. I had attended school on Friday only so I'd be eligible to play in the basketball game on Saturday. Once we were on the court, we dominated the other team. We were winning by thirty points, but the coach still wanted us to be aggressive. After I got a rebound, a kid from the other team grabbed the ball to cause a jump ball. After the referee blew the whistle, I ripped the ball out of his hands, and the kid retaliated and pushed me.

I felt the anger swell up inside. I punched him in the face. Spit flew from his mouth, and blood trickled from his lip. The referees pulled us apart, and one of them said, "Technical foul. You're out of the game." But I felt no sympathy, no remorse.

As I walked, furious, toward my head coach, he screamed, "What the hell you doing?"

I screamed, "Fuck you!" and threw a chair to half court before storming out of the gymnasium. I kicked the door open and ran out of the building. My parents ran after me, but I continued to run down the steep hill in front of the school. I ripped off my jersey and threw it in the air. I knew I wanted nothing to do with St. Stephan's. I don't think I had ever been that mad in my life—and I'd been *mad*. I felt ready to kill.

My parents tried to wrestle me to the ground, and I pinned them to the ground with ease despite my diminished frame. I got up and continued running and evading my parents while screaming at the top of my lungs. I wasn't screaming words; I was letting out a primal roar as if the beast inside me was finally coming out. My head pounded and my heart raced.

Soon, I became tired, and my softer emotions took over. All the frustration and pent-up sadness seemed to pour out in the form of tears. A flurry of emotions was happening inside. I was on an adrenaline high from the game, but I knew I was losing myself and who I was before my illness.

I finally calmed down enough for my parents to talk to me. Once they were able to talk me down, my dad carried me to the car, and we went home.

Chapter 11
The Damage Is Deeper

After my outburst at the game, everything was a mess. For the next few days, my parents fielded phone calls from concerned parents who said they wanted to tell the vicious basketball coach the same two words I had.

Some of my classmates' parents were genuinely concerned about me, which gave me some reassurance that they legitimately cared about me. It let me know I had people on my side ready to help. I felt I was being more fully supported after having received my diagnosis. Though the administration at school was no longer my ally, I was gaining a small army of supporters.

I slept for the remainder of the weekend and into the next week. My parents allowed me to stay home from school to let me recuperate from the episode a few days earlier. On Wednesday of that week, my dad came down to my room in the basement. He approached me timidly as to not inspire another outburst. "The antibiotics are working, but they will take time," he said. "You'll get worse before you get better." I hated to hear this phrase more than anything. "And we still need you to go to school."

He looked at me with genuine concern. "Your mom and I have talked to Sr. Renee, and she's willing to let you take a few months off from St. Stephan's and go to public school at Coelho where they can give you the accommodations you need."

That confused me. "Why won't Sr. Renee let me have half days?"

My father looked defeated. "They cannot make any accommodations for you. St. Stephan's is a private Catholic school. They don't have to make any."

Why couldn't I come in late or have a modified schedule? I began to cry. I felt like I'd given the school so much. They'd gotten so much good press from the electric car, and now they were throwing me out with the garbage. I was upset because I couldn't control my outbursts. But I was at that point facing the consequences. After crying for several minutes, I screamed at the top of my lungs and starting hitting things. After I was exhausted from blazing another path of destruction, I fell asleep.

While I was on the antibiotics, outbursts like those got only worse. I was mad at everyone; I just wanted things to go back to the way they had been. I didn't know why all of these terrible things were happening to me, and I still didn't realize how bad my outbursts really were. When one happened, I went to another place in my mind. Later, my memory of it would be fuzzy at best.

When the anger overtook me, I screamed cuss words while kicking, punching, and throwing anything in my way, including people and things. I ripped the kitchen drawers apart searching for a knife or anything sharp. If I found one, I picked it up and screamed, "I'm going to fucking kill you!" All the while, I was somewhere else, unaware and out of control. I was possessed.

While in these fits of rage, I had a fuzzy consciousness. My parents had to get rid of all the knives in the house. Despite my general unawareness, there were times I do remember. Once, I was furious with Alicia probably over some frivolous thing, and I picked up a knife. When my dad held me back, I threw it at her. It sliced her arm open.

I didn't want to face my life. I knew St. Stephan's couldn't do anything for me, but I knew I could go back there if I got better. Still unsure about how to handle everything that was going on in my life, I just slept. After I spent about two weeks living on the couch, my dad woke me up one afternoon and told me I was going to start at Coelho in the next few days. He said I would go in only for a math class because it was my worst subject, and then I would have a tutor for an hour after school.

I had never been to a public school. The biggest class I had ever been in was a class of thirty kids, but the public school had two hundred per class. At St. Stephan's I was in a class of seventeen; I had no idea what to expect at my new school. I had always gone to a Catholic school that required uniforms, so I didn't have many other clothes.

At eleven one night, after I woke up from a nearly thirty-hour slumber, my dad took me to get some new clothes. I was exhausted and didn't want to be there. The lights nearly blinded me, and I didn't have the energy to shop. I trudged through the aisles, leaning heavily on the steel-shopping cart. I rifled through the racks, picked out a few T-shirts and jeans, and went home.

The next day, my dad had to drag me out of bed at noon to take me for a tour of Coelho Middle School. We met the vice principal, Mrs. Knox. The short, dark-haired, woman was very pleasant and welcoming. She took me around to all the classrooms and showed me where my locker would be. The size of the school was what shocked me the most. St. Stephan's had 500 students while Coelho had 1,200. It seemed to take forever to tour the school. However, the biggest shock came when the bell rang and the students changed classes. There was not a uniform in sight; each student was dressed differently. That made me fearful since I had always gone to a Catholic school. *What will the other kids think of me?* That was when it really hit me that I was actually going to have to go to school in this place. Not that I had anything against the school itself, but I was adamant that I was going to graduate from St. Stephan's, and I fully intended to do so.

As I was given my locker number, I thought that I already had a locker at St. Stephan's with all my books in it and my laptop for student council meetings. The realization felt heavy, but I knew all that would be there for me when I transferred back after a few months. Going back to St. Stephan's was my only motivation to do well at Coelho. So I went with the mentality that this was a short-term thing. I decided I would be back at St. Stephan's by Valentine's Day at the latest—that was the date I had started at St. Stephan's four years earlier. I marked the date on my calendar and knew if I kept my eye on the prize, I could achieve my goal of graduating from St. Stephan's. It was November 14; I knew that in three months I would be able to fully recover and go back to the school I loved, so I was optimistic.

After my tour of Coelho, my parents and I had a meeting with the principal, the vice principal, and the school nurse. The nurse said, "I have been researching Lyme disease all night, and it's fascinating. I cannot imagine what you're going through. If you ever need anything during the day, you can come to my office."

That was the first time I thought that anyone outside my family, Sue included, treated Lyme as an actual illness rather than a mental disorder. She was compassionate and sympathetic and provided a lifeline for me in my new school.

The next day was my first day of school. I was scheduled to attend one class a day and have a tutor come to my house for an hour after school. I walked into my math class and was greeted by my teacher, Mr. Nolan, with whom I went to church. The fact that I knew my teacher alleviated some of the stress of the situation and helped ease my transition to a school where I knew very few people. I felt like a kindergartener clutching a Superman lunchbox and anxiously shuffling into the first day school. When I stepped into class, Mr. Nolan introduced me. "Everyone, this is Pat. He's the new student I've been telling you about."

Everyone stared at me blankly.

"You can have a seat at that back table," Mr. Nolan whispered to me.

As I awkwardly maneuvered around chairs and desks, every student continued to stare at me—I thought, *I don't belong here.* I recognized one kid at my table from my recreational baseball league, but I had never talked to him. One of the students in our cluster surprised me by introducing himself. "Hi. I'm Scott."

I was taken aback that he had introduced himself.

"Hi. I'm Pat," I said quietly.

"What school did you come from?"

"St. Stephan's in Rhode Island."

"I've never heard of it. You'll like it here much better, though."

"I really hope so."

"So you're coming to school only for math?"

I realized Mr. Nolan had already told the class my story. "Yeah."

"What about all your other subjects?"

"I'll have a tutor come to my house."

"That's not too bad. When I had surgery last year, I had a tutor come to my house, and I caught up in no time."

"Yeah, I hope I can catch up too."

"But hey, it could be worse, man. If you need anything, we're here for you."

This was an incredible feeling. Not only was Scott empathetic; he also seemed to genuinely care about me. I quickly realized that all the other students accepted me just like any other kid—I hadn't expected that. Without even realizing it, I had stereotyped the public school kids as poor and stupid, not good enough to pay for school. But from my first day at Coelho, I was learning I needed to rethink my assumptions; the students there were so much more genuine, caring, and down to earth than all the kids I'd ever met at the two Catholic schools I'd attended.

After the first few days, I became more comfortable with my new school. *Maybe this could really be a fresh start.* It was still difficult for me to get up in the morning, but my dad would start trying to wake me up at 10:30 each morning. As my multiple alarms blasted, he always started by turning the lights on and ripping off my covers. After about a half hour of that, he'd wrestle me out of bed, and I would lie on the floor for a while. Finally, I made it to the bathroom after he started the shower for me. I then locked the door and slept on the bathroom floor for about half an hour. Afterward, I took my extra pillow and blanket from the bathroom closet and slept for about another hour still on the bathroom floor.

No matter what we did, I just couldn't get up. No amount of determination or drive could lift me from my slumber. My dad proved his unconditional love for me by putting that much effort into simply getting me out of bed.

The regimen of five antibiotics I was on made me even more tired than I was before my diagnosis. It seemed as if everyone told me, "You'll get worse before you get better." This was exactly what I didn't want to hear. While the Herxheimer effect ran its course, I felt as though I were slowly dying. I wanted both my time at Coelho and my Lyme recovery to be short bouts, although in the back of my mind, I probably knew they would last much longer. I tried to make the best of it.

After the first couple of days, it seemed everyone in school knew who I was. I was in one class with about twenty kids, but all the other kids were equally as nice as those I had first met. I finally felt like I was being treated as a normal person instead of a psychopath. I wasn't ostracized and excluded for my differences. I was accepted for my personality and who I was behind my symptoms. I soon realized that there were many students like Scott who could empathize with my situation. They didn't completely understand what I was going through, but I quickly learned everyone goes through undesirable stuff at some point.

That made it impossible to be judgmental; you never know what someone's story really is.

However, there was some bad with the good. I did see some drug use and fighting. A girl claimed she had been raped in the bathroom, and though the court found the boy not guilty, the school was in the news; my previous school was only in the news for the electric car. Finally, there was a bomb threat at the school, and the school was shut down for the day. The students realized that if they sent in bomb threats, they'd get the day off, so over the next few weeks, four or five of them were called in. When a police officer came to our school and told us that we could be arrested for doing that, the threats ended.

These incidents were very different and scary for me because I had never experienced anything like them before. As crazy as it might sound, I'm glad these types of things happened because they opened my eyes to the real world. I was terrified at the time, but in retrospect, I'm glad I experienced them. I had been sheltered behind Catholic school conduct and uniforms for my entire life with the same twenty or thirty kids from the same background and socioeconomic status—always Catholic, white kids. I'd been oblivious to the school and living conditions that were only a mile away from my home. Coelho also taught me to be grateful for what I had. My experiences helped me realize that gratitude is understanding there's always someone better off than you and always someone worse off than you.

When I viewed my situation from my new perspective, I realized I didn't really have it that bad. Though I was sicker than I had ever been, sometimes even feeling on the verge of death, at least I had a home and loving parents. I had clean clothes to wear to school and food to eat when I got there, a luxury many students at Coelho didn't have.

By December, after I had settled into my new school, I was struggling with math. I was in pre-algebra, the lowest level that was offered, but I was still struggling to pass. I was not the only one in the class who was struggling; four of us needed some extra help. A few days a week, during our class period, we worked with the special-needs teacher. We took all our tests with this teacher. We were allowed to use calculators and read questions aloud. I felt very belittled by that, but I realized and learned to accept that it was all part of the significant impact Lyme disease had had on my brain.[6] I didn't know how much I struggled neurologically until I had gone from being an honor roll student at St. Stephan's, whose curriculum was extremely challenging, to a special-needs class in the lowest level class offered.

Though my life was changing rapidly, I still had one glimmer of hope from my previous life: Jarred Lorrusso. For my birthday, Jarred invited me to go to an Avenged Sevenfold concert with him. I liked the band but had never really got into them; however, it was one of his favorites, so I decided to go with him. Jarred, his girlfriend, and I went up to Lowell, Massachusetts, for the concert, about an hour and twenty-five minutes from my house. Our tickets were for the mosh pit, and that frightened me a little because of my Lyme-induced claustrophobia. I didn't want to be in elevators or tight spaces—they caused episodes similar to the one I'd had with video games. But I didn't want to ruin their time, so I just went along with it, hoping everything would be fine.

Through the opening acts, I was fine and had a great time. But once Avenged Sevenfold came on, more people crowded into the mosh pit. I felt trapped. The lights turned off, and the laser show began. At first, the lights and lasers just bugged my eyes, but I ignored my twitching eyes and headache. As the show went on, I started feeling nauseous and like I was going to faint. The subtle twitching in my eyes became uncontrollable, and I started to lose feeling in my arms and legs; I felt I was floating. Everything started to slow down, and even though we were about twenty feet from the roaring speakers, I couldn't hear anything. The blaring music turned into muffled, slow-motion background noise. All the colors of the light show and the people around me became distorted and blurred. I passed out.

The next thing I remembered was Jarred shaking me in slow motion. He was screaming in my face, but I couldn't hear him. I was crowd-surfed out of the mosh pit and taken out by security guards. They stood me up and expected me to walk away, thinking I was just another crowd surfer. I had no idea what was going on. I walked two steps and fell flat on my face. The next thing I knew, I was in a security office, handcuffed to a chair with a nurse taking my blood pressure.

Several police officers questioned me about what I had drunk or if I had taken any drugs. I was still out of it, and my speech was slurred. I smelled like alcohol and marijuana from having been in the mosh pit, but I hadn't drunk or smoked anything. They gave me a breathalyzer, which came back negative, but they still thought I must have been high on something.

The police officers said that they'd call my parents to tell them I was being arrested for underage intoxication and that they could pick me up at the Lowell police station. Unable to speak, I pulled my phone from my pocket and gave it to an officer. While that was happening, the nurse took my blood pressure. She called the EMTs over when it read 180/120. She said she had checked my blood pressure three times and it continued to rise; that was an emergency. The officer who was already on the phone with my mom started yelling into the phone and demanding her to tell him what medications I was on. She told him I was suffering from Lyme disease, and that opened up a whole new can of worms.

I went from being a typical teenager at a concert who probably had had too much to drink to being in a life-threatening crisis. They put me on a stretcher and rushed out of the arena. My vision was distorted, but as I passed by, I heard countless people saying, "Oh my God! What's wrong with him? Look at his eyes." Apparently, my eyes were rolling back into my head.

As they put me in the ambulance, I felt my heart rate getting higher and higher. I blacked out for a second time on the way to the hospital. While I was still semi-conscious, I saw a foggy image of an EMT waving a flashlight in my eyes and felt him shaking me violently. I blacked out completely before being jolted awake. I was gasping for air. I thought I was about to die. I began to panic because I wasn't sure what was happening. I went into shock.

Many doctors and nurses were waiting for me when we arrived at the hospital; that was when I knew something was wrong. They started ripping my clothes off and putting all kinds of monitors on my chest and head. After receiving several IV bags and injections, I began to calm down. After about an hour, I began to come out of my catatonic state, but I felt disoriented and light-headed. I had no idea what had happened.

I called my parents. They asked multiple times if I'd taken anything or had been drinking, and I kept saying no. When they arrived later, they were extremely happy to see me. The nurse told them I'd had two seizures—once at the concert and a second in the ambulance. After doing some follow-up tests, I was discharged. We left, my parents pushing me in a wheelchair to the car.

I saw Sue immediately after this incident for some advice about our course of action. After the concert, I began having focal seizures about once a week. I'd stare blankly into space completely unaware of what was happening similar to the issue with the video games about a year before. The seizures weren't the only problem: The hour of school and hour of tutoring were becoming increasingly challenging for me, and I struggled to keep up. I struggled to focus while I read; my eyes twitched, and I constantly had blurred vision. When I told Sue, she recommended that I have a neuropsychological evaluation and eye exam to figure out exactly why the episode at the concert had happened.

After several weeks of waiting, we got an appointment with a renowned neurophysiologist. He specialized in brain injuries and patients suffering from tick-borne illnesses. After a tedious and exhausting three-day test that included memory, eye tracking, handwriting, reading, neuromuscular function capabilities, and cognitive testing, and just when I was about to walk out the door, the doctor called my mom into his office. I sat in the waiting room just outside, so I heard the majority of their conversation. My jaw dropped when I hear him say, "He's reading and writing at a first-grade level, which is why it's so hard for him to perform in school. I don't see it likely in his future for him to ever go back to school full-time again."

At first, I was angry and in disbelief. I was ready to break down the door and give him a piece of my mind. But my anger suddenly dissolved, and I was struck with fear that my brain would be this way for the rest of my life. I found a seat in the waiting room. I held back my tears and stared at the floor, thinking over and over, *This cannot be happening.*

After about two hours of discussion with the doctor, my mom finally came out of his office. Her eyes were red and puffy. We said our good-byes and left. My mom filled me in on the drive home. The neuropsychologist said my eye-tracking ability was greatly diminished and that it would be very difficult for me to play sports. I was stunned. Several other doctors had also told me I would never play sports again, but it finally seemed real.

After her talk with the doctor, my mom was more concerned than ever. The conversation had taught her that my disease was real and the direct cause of my academic ineptitude. She believed that Lyme was real and she believed that chronic Lyme was real, but that was a poignant moment for her; she realized the damage my disease had done to my brain.

After the nephrologist, my psychologist, and various other primary care givers had received the results of my exam, they unanimously concluded that I should stay with the hour of tutoring or be home schooled for the rest of my academic career. I knew I was struggling, but I didn't think the situation was that dire. Yes, the seizure at the concert was terrifying, but I thought I'd be able to work through my academic struggles.

Not only did my ailment finally have a name, but I then knew it had also destroyed my mental capacity possibly beyond recovery. The issue I'd been confident I would overcome was far more severe than previously anticipated. The damage was deeper than anyone had thought. But I knew that the results of my neuropsyc didn't lie, and I felt powerless as my disease took a firm clutch on my life.

We were determined to discover to what extent the Lyme had affected my brain. I had been previously unable to have an MRI with contrast because I had braces. But I got them off in December two weeks after the concert, Sue had me go for a SPECT scan, which is a form of imaging that uses radioactive contrast to create a 3-D picture of the brain. That was the only way to see if the Lyme had affected the brain. When the results came back, I was speechless.

During this appointment, I sat silently on the table. A doctor came bursting into the room and said, "Good morning, Patrick," and shook my hand. "I have the results of your SPECT scan, and it isn't good." He was talking quickly. He whipped out two X-rays and shoved them up into the lightboard. "This is what a normal brain looks like," he said pointing to one. "And this is what your brain looks like." He pointed to the other. "You see all these spots?"

"Yes," I said quietly.

"These are lesions. You have seven large ones, and they're all over your brain. This is what's causing all your difficulties in school and your seizures. As long as the Lyme is in your brain, it will continue to deteriorate your brain tissue. They will most likely only get worse."

My dad was fidgety in his chair. "Will they ever get better?"

"It's really hard to say," the doctor said. "We'll have to wait and see. Let's do another scan in about six months and see if there's any progress."

"What does he do about school?" my dad asked.

The doctor grimaced and refused to look my dad in the eye. "School isn't his priority right now." He spoke as if I weren't in the room. But then he looked at me. "You need to focus on recovering right now and nothing else. You have to understand that the lesions severely impair your brain function."

I felt defeated. My stomach began to turn in knots. Normally, I remained silent during my appointments, but I needed to speak up. "So what am I supposed to do?" I began to tear up.

"I'm not sure if I know what you mean."

"When do you think that I will be able to go back to school full-time?"

He laughed. "Like I said, school isn't your priority right now. Be kind to yourself. You've been through a lot. But this damage could be permanent."

My dad interjected, "So will he ever recover?"

"I don't know much about Lyme," the doctor said, "but from what I can see, it will be very difficult for his brain to heal."

"What about sports?" I pleaded.

He smirked again. He was becoming frustrated. He spoke more loudly than before. "You won't go back to school full-time or play sports again. You essentially have holes in your brain. I don't see you making a recovery anytime soon."

I found comfort in the fact that these scans proved that I hadn't been faking my symptoms, but the news weighed heavily on my parents and me. I felt the doctor's sympathy, but it didn't make me feel better. How is one supposed to give this news to a fourteen-year-old? This doctor, who had known me for all of twenty minutes, had no idea what it was like to have his words become my destiny. He didn't know that I was born a fighter.

My parents were more in denial than anything else. They were more concerned with getting me happy and healthy again than getting me back to school. All they wanted was the vibrant, happy-go-lucky son they used to have.

I was overwhelmed. I accepted this diagnosis as permanent. I felt I couldn't fight anymore. I let the words of the medical professionals make up my mind for me that it was the end. What choice did I have? I couldn't change what was happening, and the doctors couldn't either. If a doctor said something, it was true. I couldn't have been a more average kid before I contracted Lyme disease, but I felt at that point that my life was over. I accepted the results as a death sentence. I had to go to school only until I was eighteen, and then I would sleep in my parents' house for the rest of my life, slowly draining them of all their resources. I had no purpose. If there was a God, why had He let this happen? Didn't He care? Couldn't He help? I guessed not.

I decided to let Lyme slowly kill me.

Chapter 12
Making a Final Choice

"You won't go to school full-time or play sports again." Every day, about fifty times a day, I would replay those words in my mind. With each repetition of this phrase, I fell into deeper depression. My life as a "normal" person was over. However, my parents did their best to treat me as they always did, as if this news hadn't come. Every day they sat with me and talked to me though I was in a deep sleep.

I had no hope or purpose, and I continued to feel awful. I had seizures and emotional breakdowns. I was put on Mepron, a cyst-busting drug to help get the Lyme out of my brain and repair the lesions. It came in a vulgar-tasting, yellow, paint-like solution. It made me feel only worse. My brain felt even more unclear, and my body aches and anger worsened. Every morning and night, my dad would come to my room, pour the medicine into my mouth, and force me to swallow. I knew it made me worse, so I tried not to take it. Being on this new medicine made me feel even more useless to my family due to the excessive cost.

Mepron is referred to as liquid gold in the Lyme community because insurance doesn't cover it for Lyme disease. It can cost up to $1,000 per bottle. My parents had spent upward of $80,000 on medicines, doctors, and tests that were not covered by insurance, taken mostly from their education and retirement funds, and all I did was sleep all day. Through my troubled sleep, I heard my parents arguing with each other or over the phone with an insurance company agent about whether chronic Lyme disease exists. Even times when I was feeling well, I ended up hurting my family with the financial burden my disease had created. The constant arguments about money made me feel more burdensome.

I didn't know what to do about all that, so I tried to hide, to isolate myself, to pretend none of it was happening. But the pressure was building. I was a danger to everyone around me, and more so to myself. I tried to miss as many days of school at Coelho as I could because I knew that was the way it would probably be for the rest of my life or at least until I was eighteen. I stopped doing schoolwork. *What's the point? I'll never be able to go back to school full-time anyway.*

This led to many dark days of not talking to anyone. I went days in a row without saying a word. I became numb and felt lost. During the days I spent staring off into space at home, I began to wonder if I should kill myself. This escalated from passing thoughts of *If I die, I won't be in pain anymore* to wondering how I would do it. I struggled constantly with those thoughts. My first thought was, *I'll shoot myself,* but I realized I couldn't get a gun. *Maybe I'll hang myself.* But I didn't have rope and didn't feel I had the physical strength to climb high enough.

One day after school, I was home alone. I was so desperate to die that I decided to stab myself in the stomach. I went to the kitchen and grabbed the biggest knife I could find. I held the tip of the knife below my sternum. The garage door opened. I put the knife away and went to lie down. I realized it would be harder than I thought. I continued to live my life in misery.

My parents noticed that I had been unusually despondent. They correctly assumed that it was due to the news I'd received. They sent me to several therapists, including a counselor who specialized in Lyme disease and had it herself, but I never really opened up to her. I never talked to the counselors and therapists because I knew they couldn't have had any idea what I was going through. Even the Lyme therapist didn't understand the severity of my problems. She had been able to work through Lyme, and she didn't understand what was happening to my mind. I was glad she could empathize with my Lyme symptoms, but she had something that I didn't—the perseverance and motivation to work through it.

While the doctors' words about my future resonated in my mind, there was a deeper question that was even harder to accept. What kind of so-called loving God would put one of His children through such pain and suffering? I had abandoned my faith long before that. I was on bad terms with God. Every night before bed, I asked Him one last favor: please take me from this earth and from my misery. When I woke up every morning, I doubted God even more. Every night after what I called my "prayer," I stuck my middle finger in the air and cursed the God who had put me where I was.

Typical words of encouragement people offered me throughout that time consisted of "Bad things happen for a reason." But to me, that was a kick in the teeth. If all bad things happen for a reason, that meant God intended suffering to happen. That meant God gave me Lyme disease and forced me to go through all my suffering. I started to believe God was causing my pain, and that made me feel even more alone. I felt I'd never be relieved of my pain. I believed the world would be a much better, happier place without me in it.

One day, my parents woke me up and told me I had another doctor's appointment. *Fine*, I thought. *But there's nothing more that can be done for me.* I expected the same old waste of time, but what did I care? My time was a waste anyway.

Dr. Fredric Silverblatt was an infectious disease doctor. He never took pediatric cases, but our family friend, the nephrologist, called in a favor after he saw firsthand how much I was suffering, and he felt guilty he'd been unable to help me after nearly fifty years of being a part of my family's life.

The doctor walked into the room, and I wanted to laugh because he looked about seventy-five and was wearing a purple, polka-dot bowtie. He began with the usual tests that all the doctors had subjected me to. He checked my reflexes and looked into my eyes and down my throat. But when he was looking into my ears, I heard him humming. He was vibrant. He seemed happy to be working with me. His personality was different from those of the cold, indifferent doctors I'd seen previously.

"So how long have you been sick for?"

"About two years."

He looked at me with concern. "I'm sorry to hear that. Let's see if we can't make you feel any better."

He continued to question me about my disease. I wasn't used to that; my other doctors had usually spoken just with my parents. I felt he cared. I felt human. I told him everything I could. I told him about the brain scans and that the other doctor said I wouldn't go back to school full-time again.

The other doctor's prognosis struck a nerve with Dr. Silverblatt. He shook his head, took his glasses off, and stood. "Patrick, I know how badly you're suffering because I was in the same boat." He had my attention. He put his hand on my shoulder. I felt accepted and comforted. "Four years ago, I couldn't feed myself or even read a clock. I was almost crippled, and my hands were so swollen that I couldn't even write out my own checks."

A part of me didn't believe him; he seemed fine at the time. But he continued. "I went to every doctor there was and tried every medicine, but nothing helped me. Doctors told me the same thing—that I would never be able to work again and I should retire. But I believed I could recover. Nothing helped more than one simple thing." He came closer and whispered, "Exercise."

"Wait … what?" I heard him, but the thought seemed crazy.

"Exercise," he repeated.

"What did you say?" my mom asked.

He chuckled. "Exercise. You know, like biking, walking, running," he said sarcastically.

I began to think this man was a lunatic. I was shocked, and I scoffed at the idea. I was hardly able to walk the few hundred steps from the car to his office and he expected me to exercise? I thought he was crazy.

"How could that help him?" my mom nervously asked.

"If you start to exercise, it doesn't matter how simple or for how long, it will make you feel better. Moving will help your joints and body feel better, sweating will get the toxins of the Lyme out of your body, and it will make the antibiotics go to your brain and work much more quickly."

He told me he'd ridden his bike for fifteen minutes a day, and he'd seen better results from a month of that than he had from two years of antibiotics. I couldn't believe what he was saying. I had thousands of dollars' worth of antibiotics traveling through my veins and Dr. Silverblatt was trying to convince me my cure was free?

Nevertheless, his story gave me hope, but I thought I could never exercise. I was beyond hope. The hope that he had given me dissolved by the time I reached the stairs outside of the office. My first step down sent pain throughout my whole body, and my breath was labored. *There's no way I can exercise.* My joints and body simply hurt too badly. My head pounded, and I was light-headed. My ears rang even if I walked too fast. The man wanted me to spend the half an hour a day that I was awake torturing my body even more. I wrote him off as crazy.

I went back home, depressed and tired. I rejected the hope Dr. Silverblatt offered, but I cooked up my own plan. I thought back to when I started to go to school at St. Stephan's in fourth grade after my concussion. *If they accepted me then, injured and behind, they'll accept me now*, I thought. It was the end of January, so that gave me about three weeks to pull myself together and return to St. Stephan's.

I marked my calendar with the days until February 14. I started going back to the hour of school and tutoring again after not having done that for over a month. I envisioned my future: I'd go back to St. Stephan's and be with all my friends and favorite teachers and everything would be normal again—the way it used to be as if nothing had happened. I posted on Facebook about my goal, and my friends gave me words of encouragement.

When there was about a week left, I told my dad about my countdown. He brushed it off. "No, they can't take you back until you start going full days again." But I kept on counting down, sure that once this awful disease was over, I could start a new chapter in my life. I convinced myself that they would take me back. I truly believed if I just showed up again, everything would be okay. I was ready to fight and start fresh with St. Stephan's despite my past behavior. I knew if they just gave me another chance, I'd be able to pull myself together and go full days again.

On February 13, 2010, I picked up my phone and anxiously began typing with arthritic fingers. I texted all my friends from St. Stephan's to tell them I was coming back the next day. I laid my uniform out for the morning. I was ready to go. My dad came down to my room to say goodnight and asked me why I had my uniform out.

"Because I'm going back to St. Stephan's tomorrow," I said, pulling out my calendar to show him the date as if my writing on the calendar was significant.

He looked down. He swallowed hard as if the words were unable to come out of his throat. Finally, he put his hand on his forehead as if he realized he'd made a mistake. He said, "You can't go back. They don't want you."

"They don't want me?" I was shocked "What do you mean? St. Stephan's is a part of who I am. What do you mean they don't want me?"

"I should have told you this sooner," my dad said slowly. "They sent us a letter a few months ago after your outburst with your basketball coach saying that they couldn't accommodate you and that they thought you'd be best off if you finished out the year at Coelho."

I started sobbing. "I don't believe you. Show me the letter. There's no way they could just kick me out. I have done everything for that school!"

My dad went upstairs and came back down with the letter. As he read the letter to me, my anger rose. Several lines stood out: "It seems to me that Patrick's special needs would be best supported at Coelho for the duration of the year" and "His safety and the welfare of our students come first in the decision we have made." That was it. They weren't required by law to accommodate me, and they wouldn't.

But the Sisters of Mercy were founded on the principles of providing education for those who were sick or in need. Who was sicker or more in need than I was?

My dad felt the same way. He showed me a four-page response he'd sent to Sr. Renee, which included,

> The Sisters of Mercy is an international community of Roman Catholic women who have vowed to serve people who suffer from poverty, sickness, and lack of education with a special concern for women and children. Given the fact that St. Stephan's is run by the Sisters of Mercy, I would like you to honestly take an examination of conscience and see if allowing Patrick to attend school only if he can attend on a full-time basis exhibits the *spirit* of the Sisters of Mercy. Are you really serving children who are sick? Patrick has a tick-borne illness, which he most likely contracted on a school-sponsored trip. He came home sick from camp and was not diagnosed until this fall with Lyme and Bartonella.

What if he had brain cancer? Would you handle the
situation in the same manner?

Actions like that made me love my father even more, and they exemplified
the unconditional love and support he gave me throughout my battle.

My dad left to go upstairs; he knew I needed time alone. My emotions
boiled up. First sadness, blubbering, and sobbing and then resentment
and anger. I looked around my room to see all the awards on my walls
I had received from building the electric car. They all said St. Stephan's
Academy on them. My name was synonymous with theirs. I ripped the
five or six plaques and certificates off the wall and threw them across
the room. My swearing mixed with the sound of shattering glass. I did
the same with my St. Stephan's Academy basketball trophies. I was
disgusted; I couldn't bear to see the name St. Stephan. "Why the fuck
do they not want me? I've done everything for them! No one would
know about that school if it weren't for me!" I screamed as I raged
uncontrollably.

I began whaling away at my punching bag. I felt justified because
of hypocritical actions of the administration of St. Stephan's and by Sr.
Renee. After the punching bag no longer served as a viable surrogate, I
punched a hole in my wall. Then I began pounding on the door to try to
get my dad to set me free. He tried to contain the beast that had escaped
from inside me, but there was no stopping my rage.

My throat was sore from yelling, my eyes hurt from crying, and
my hands were bruised from punching the walls and door. After all my
aggression was out and I had lost my voice from the yelling, I collapsed,
a desolate being. My dad came in to comfort me. When I ran out of
tears, I went over to my computer. I googled my name, and my picture
with Jarred, Mr. M, and the electric car in front of St. Stephan's was the
first thing that came up. I couldn't believe I was the poster child for the
school but it would just kick me out as if I were nothing. Mine was the
first picture to come up on the homepage of their website, but to them,
I was no more than a publicity stunt and a paycheck. I was hysterical,
hyperventilating, and sobbing.

I thought my life was over—again. Going back to St. Stephan's
was the only inspiration I had to try to get better; without that, I was

crushed. I fell asleep in my dad's arms. Maybe when I woke up, I thought, everything would be back to normal. Maybe it was all a nightmare. Maybe my entire illness was some kind of sick dream or demented illusion.

My dad woke me up about ten-thirty the next morning to go to my hour of school at Coelho.

"Patrick, wake up. Time for school."

"At St. Stephan's, yes." Though I was in a sleepy haze, I was in denial.

My dad was frustrated with my desire to go back. "You can't go back. They don't want you. They kicked you out. There's nothing you can do about it!" He didn't understand why I felt such a strong connection to the school.

He picked me up out of bed, and I started shoving and punching him, screaming, "I'm going back! I have done everything for them! I don't care I made that school what it is now, and they can't just fucking kick me out!"

He came back and tried to grab me; I kicked him square in the chest, knocking him to the ground.

He'd had enough. He wrestled me and pinned me down, and he screamed in my face, "You really are fucking crazy!" In my whole life, my dad had never laid a hand on me or yelled at me like that. *I'm not the only one who's changed.*

The fighting continued for several hours until my dad realized I was too emotionally distressed to go to school that day, so he let me stay home. I spent the whole day crying. I didn't realize it was possible to cry so much or be so sad. I was more alone than I'd ever been. I learned what rock bottom felt like.

What had been recurring dark thoughts before now had the heft of facts: my entire world was shattered. I had nothing to live for. I had nothing left to contribute to the world. I would never go to school or play sports again. I would never read or write again. Even the letter that had devastated me so completely needed to be read to me. I spent the day in total darkness. I kept thinking, *Why could it not be cancer? Then, people would actually care about me.*

But I wanted more than for people to care about me. I needed someone else to listen.

"God, if there is a God, just take me out of my misery. Let me die in my sleep so I don't have to be a burden to my family anymore." I knew that if there were a God, He would not make me suffer the way I was suffering. Every morning I woke up affirmed my belief there was no God.

After several pensive hours, I made a decision. God couldn't help me, so I would help myself. I decided to kill myself. I wrote a note in what scribbled handwriting I could force, telling my parents and sisters that I loved them and that this was for their own good. "This world will be a much better and happier place without me in it," I wrote.

I decided to take whatever pills I could find. I swallowed a bottle of Advil one pill at a time. Each pill represented a different pain in my life—a person, a situation, a physical pain. One for every doctor who told me I would never amount to anything. One for every outburst. One for every time I needed to fight back tears and conceal my symptoms. I thought the pills would symbolically make it better while they slowly killed me. After I finished the bottle of sixty Advil, I lay on my bed, staring at the ceiling and waiting to die. After a few minutes, all the pills had done was make my chest a little heavy and my heart beat faster. *I can't do anything right*, I thought. I was nothing. I could accomplish nothing. I couldn't even kill myself the right way, but I wasn't giving up. I was on Doxycycline, which I was not supposed to mix with dairy, so I took the entire bottle of Doxycycline, each pill one by one, and washed it down with about half a gallon of milk.

I wanted to die. As I became light-headed, I knew I was getting close, so I moved on to sleeping pills. The sleeping pills represented laying to rest not only myself but also all the pain I had experienced during my battle with Lyme. My hope was that my family would find the note and would hope I had died peacefully in my sleep. I thought that if cause of death on my death certificate was listed as Lyme disease, people might start looking at the disease more seriously. I took the sleeping pills by the handful, not wasting any time.

After the second handful, I felt my heart racing and my head pounding. I could no longer feel my arms or legs, and my extremities began shaking erratically. I felt blood pulsing through my eyes as if they were going to burst from their sockets. I knew it was the end. My stomach was in knots and felt like it was on fire. Then I began vomiting uncontrollably. The vomit laced with blood covered my bed and body.

I had been warned continuously not to take my doxycycline with dairy because it could burn holes in my organs. I realized that is what had happened. It felt like my stomach acid was dissolving my throat and esophagus. I tried to scream for help, but I couldn't make a sound. My whole body started shaking, and my heart was pumping faster than it ever had. It was the most pain I had ever felt. My throat closed, and it felt like a thousand knives were stabbing me. I was sure it was all over, and there was no turning back, but my situation provoked a fight-or-flight reaction. My desire to die dissipated. I didn't want to feel pain.

I wanted to call 911, but I was unable to reach my phone. I started convulsing and could no longer breathe. My heart continued pounding in my ears, and I was sure I'd die. I'd thought pills meant dying wouldn't be painful. After every muscle in my body had locked up and I could no longer move, after the vomit flooded my throat and blood rushed from every orifice of my being, it was all just over.

All the pain suddenly stopped, and everything went silent. My pain morphed into euphoria. I felt I was floating as I left my body. All I could see was a blinding whiteness and clouds all around me. I heard an angelic choir singing deafening high notes.

A break formed in the clouds. I saw the door to an office on the highest floor of an office building; the door read "Patrick Collins." As I reached for the knob, the door opened. I walked past a receptionist's desk and waiting room. I knew this was an actual experience, not a dream—it was too vivid. I wasn't worried. I was experiencing what heaven was like.

I continued into the office to see an enormous desk with my name on it. I noticed an oversized leather chair and a window that provided a view of the cityscape. I examined the titles in the bookcases by the window. I sank into the leather chair and ran my fingers over the embossed arms of the chair. I felt the soft carpet under my feet.

I sat there in perfect peace and enjoyed heaven. It was perfection; I was finally at peace, no longer suffering. I was calm.

The tranquility was soon shattered by a booming voice unlike anything I had heard before. "Patrick, my child, it is not your time. Look at all I have planned for you."

I was sure this clear and articulate voice was God's and these words were true—the first words I have ever heard that were undeniably true. Unlike the words of those who doubted me—teachers, doctors, or peers—these words were sincere.

This was the first time in my life I had felt God's presence. I felt that nothing else mattered. I no longer worried about my disease, the friends who had abandoned me, or any of my other problems. I was encapsulated in pure perfection.

I woke up the next morning at four in a pool of vomit and blood. I saw the empty pill bottles all around my bed. I touched my mouth and wiped the regurgitated blood away. I felt at peace and apathetic about the chaos that surrounded me. I felt as if life was no longer real, as if every pain I had was lifted from my shoulders. Only my body had returned to this earth; all my qualms had been left somewhere else.

In that moment, I found my purpose. After I cleaned myself up, I spent several hours pondering what I had just experienced. I felt no effects from all of the pills I had just taken. I examined my body and wondered why I saw life through my own eyes. I realized that I was a singular being in the universe. I knew that only I could change my mind and state of being, and I was motivated to continue fighting and write my own story.

Of course, I questioned the legitimacy of what had happened. But I had a feeling in my heart that what I'd heard was true. The encounter I had had with God would change my life—I knew that already.

I needed to change my approach in my relationship with God. I had gained a different perspective. If everything happens for a reason, God had intended for me to suffer and lose my faith, but that wasn't true. Even if having Lyme disease was not at all a part of God's plan for me, He was there with me all the while, for God is always present.

I thought about what Dr. Silverblatt said about exercising. Knowing God had a plan for me, I was willing to try anything then. I finally had the motivation that had driven Dr. Silverblatt to overcome his Lyme disease. I realized that resiliency is not an esoteric quality; rather, it exists in us all, hidden behind our purpose in life. Once we discover our true purpose in life, nothing but ourselves can ever stop us.

My dad came down to wake me up, and he was surprised at how calm I was compared to the previous forty-eight hours. I'd cleaned up every bit of evidence. He was also shocked that I was already awake, sitting calmly. This was the first time I had woken up before 10:00 a.m. in over a year. But that was nothing compared to the shock he felt when I asked, "Can I play hockey today?"

Chapter 13
My Comeback

My recovery began at the ice rink. Even after a year's absence, my pads and skates contoured perfectly to my body. I flew around the ice thankful to be out of bed. For the first time in years, I wasn't worried. After two hours of playing and drenched in sweat, I went back to the locker room. The other guys asked if my cat had peed on my equipment because it smelled so bad. I tried to explain that was the smell of toxins and excess antibiotics leaving my body. I was so exhausted that I fell asleep in the locker room still in full equipment. I felt myself smiling because though I was physically tired, it was nothing compared to feeling that need to sleep twenty-two hours. This was not a bad kind of exhaustion; it was a feeling of accomplishment. I finally felt alive again.

There was more to life than St. Stephan's—I finally knew that. St. Stephan's was where I'd had some of the best experiences of my life, but I knew I had to move on. I was starting to see that life was all about balances: night and day, dark and light, hot and cold. You'll always have an equal number of good and bad things happen to you; it's your perception that counts. I was at my lowest point, but I was on my way up. I would use rock bottom as the sturdy foundation to build the life I would love to live.

More happened to me in two years than many people have to deal with in their entire lifetimes. God gives and takes away, and this is analogous to our life cycle as human beings. We breathe oxygen and release carbon dioxide. We reap the benefits and nutrients of the food we eat that comes from the earth, and we give those nutrients back to the earth in the form of decomposition when we die.

I had come to realize that my life and everything about it had been given to me, and since I had found God, I was determined to make the most of it. I stopped believing what the doctors told me about my future. Instead, I knew I had been put on earth to make a difference.

The following day, I went to Coelho for my hour of school. My dad had made the principal aware of my emotional struggles of the past few days, so the principal had a meeting with me to discuss what I was going through.

"I know you wanted to go back to St. Stephan's," he said, "but unfortunately, that's not what will happen. You should take this time and make the best of it. Make new friends, try new things, and experience life again."

I considered his words as I went back to class. I thought of all the friends I had and the things I liked to do before I had Lyme disease, and I remembered how great I felt then. I also thought of all the friends who thought I was crazy and had abandoned me. I decided to be more personable and approachable instead of shutting everyone out.

Over the next weeks, I started saying hi to more people and introducing myself to new people I normally wouldn't have talked to. I couldn't change the past, but I could change my outlook on life and create my future.

I had been on a treacherous road, but I could see the finish line. I was motivated by my desire to attend Bishop Feehan. I thought achieving that goal would allow me to brush off the past and create a new future. I had been given insight into my ultimate finish line during my near-death experience; I realized that death is inevitable, but I also realized I had a mission from God. Although my vision was ambiguous, it was God's proof that He hadn't planned for me to die by my own hand. My experience with God made me believe again in Him and myself. I was learning to put my life with all its ups and downs in a broader context, knowing that each incident or day is part of something bigger; seeing beyond my pain, imagining something greater.

The roller-coaster ride I called the last year of my life was analogous to the seasons in New England. I was kicked out of St. Stephan's at the end of October, and the winter that followed was brutal. After the dark, bitter, cold times when there seemed to be no hope, the sun arrived and brought warmth and sunlight in the spring, which transformed the landscape. Similarly, in my darkest hour, when I was alone praying that God would take me out of my misery, my light came, and I was changed forever.

At my next appointment with Sue about a month after my near-death experience, we discussed my persistent symptoms, and I was happy to inform her of my newfound energy and drive to exercise. That was the first improvement I'd had since I'd been diagnosed six months earlier. To build on the momentum, she wanted to put me on a PICC line, which medicated me with intravenous antibiotics. This method treated Lyme disease more quickly, especially in the brain.

In March of 2010, a PICC line was put into my left bicep leading directly into my heart. I was warned not to do any strenuous activities or lift anything over five pounds or the line could puncture an artery and cause me to bleed out.

The PICC line was the first setback to my good spirits after my experience with God. I was discouraged because I could no longer exercise as strenuously as I had in the previous few weeks, and after the line was in and I was administered my first dose, I felt no different. After failing to exercise for the next few days, my symptoms started coming back. I once again felt tired, achy, fatigued, and depressed. This was a testament to how important exercise was to my recovery. However, I was determined to get better no matter what it took. This was not like the other times during my battle when times got hard. I knew this would be hard. I kept reminding myself that things could be worse and that this was just a small setback on my road to recovery.

When I went back to Coelho, my parents and I had a meeting with Assistant Principal Knox and the nurse.

"We have had a meeting with all of the kids in your grade to tell them what you are going through and how any little push or shove could cause the line to dislodge and cause severe bleeding or death," Mrs. Knox told us. This showed me that ordinary, genuine, down-to-earth, everyday people are sometimes the most caring. My teachers, classmates, and the administration at Coelho Middle School helped me every step of the way on the road to recovery. My classmates addressed me as an actual person. I was never ostracized. My teachers understood my situation and gave me accommodations.

The road continued to be difficult, but seemingly overnight, the burden of the tantrums had been lifted. I found myself presenting myself more calmly and happier to those around me.

After the first few days of IV antibiotics, I felt more run down and was unable to even get up for my one hour of school. My dad would administer my medication while I was sleeping because I didn't have the energy to wake up. I mulled over the phrase, "You will get worse before you get better." It resonated with my current physical experience and the trajectory of my life so far; I thought I would succeed and be the best person I could be by graduating from St. Stephan's, but God had a different plan. Lyme disease destroyed the great foundation of education, friends, and memories at St. Stephan's. I was starting over, but I would be a stronger and better person because of it. I wasn't about to give up hope. God had brought me that far in my journey, and I needed to keep fighting because He would be with me all the way. I finally had hope. I finally believed I would get better.

After a month, Sue saw the progress I had made and knew I would get faster results by doubling my dose of IV antibiotics. Every other day, I received my antibiotics twice a day instead of once. My second dose was at about nine at night, and it kept me up all night. Instead of hibernating for twenty-two hours every day, I couldn't sleep much at all—the second dose of antibiotics was like a shot of adrenaline. But even on alternating days, I wasn't sleeping as late as before.

After about thirty-five days of antibiotics, I had made a complete turnaround. I finally started going back to my hour of school and felt so good that I was able to add a second and eventually a third class to my daily schedule.

I'd taught myself to shoot a hockey puck with one hand, so in mid-April, my dad took me outside with a baseball bat and asked if swinging it felt comfortable. After a few practice swings, I said yes, and he said my new baseball coach, the father of my former classmate, had called. I had never signed up to play, but the coach knew what a great player I used to be and reached out to me. The idea of playing baseball again excited me, but I wasn't sure if it would be safe because of my line.

Once a week, a nurse came to change the bandages around the PICC line to prevent infection. We proposed the idea of me playing baseball again to her, and she said it was okay. I was elated. I would finally get to play the sport I loved most, which Lyme disease had taken away from me.

We purchased a lacrosse pad and cut it in half; I wore it to protect my PICC line. The only issue I had was that I couldn't play my position—catcher—with the line in because of the required repetitive motion. I played every other position on the field, including pitcher. I was one of the top hitters on the team and did pretty well pitching.

My team, on the other hand, was a different story; we lost every game of the regular season. Even though I was a combined 3–111 for my last three seasons of baseball, I kept fighting because I loved the game. Just like my Lyme recovery, I wouldn't let one thing hold me back. A setback is nothing more than a setup for something great. Every loss I suffered in baseball made me a better player. I learned more from a loss than a win because I needed to make the adjustment and change the aspects of my game that didn't support victory.

Thanks to my newfound energy, in addition to playing baseball, I could ride my bike. I rode the same route every day, which was about fifteen miles down route 1A in North Attleboro into Wrentham, then left into Johnston. There was an extremely steep hill that was a struggle to climb every day, but I had one big piece of motivation on the other side: at the top of that treacherous hill was St. Stephan's Academy. Every day when I felt like quitting or giving up on that hill, I'd make it to the top, stop, get off my bike, look at the school, and say out loud, "Keep fighting." After that, the entire ride was downhill; I was flying and at peace with God.

Riding my bike was exercise to help get the Lyme out of my system; it also gave me time to be alone and think about my purpose in life. It seemed that I found peace only while I was riding. Climbing the hill to St. Stephan's, struggling toward my recovery, and proving the doctors wrong pushed me toward the future and kept me motivated.

Because of my exercise and sweating, my PICC line became infected and was taken out after forty-five days, on the day before Easter, which for me symbolized a new life and turning a new page. I was always taught that Jesus rose on the third day to ascend into heaven. He rose from the dead but remained on earth to serve those around Him. Through my entire struggle, the years of pain, the attempted suicide, I was now capable of exercising again—capable of fighting again. I believed in God and in myself again. I finally had the full capacity to keep fighting and beat my illness. Everyone was on my side, my parents and God included. I had been blind to that for so long, but I finally saw the light

As my life seemed to be on the upswing, so was my baseball team, the Rockies. We beat an undefeated team to begin the playoffs. Then in the championship game, I pitched three innings and got a double and a triple, driving in three of the five runs. We won 5–0.

Chapter 14
What Next?

After the triumphant underdog victory of the Attleboro Recreation Rockies, I was confident I would make a full recovery. The victory inspired me to keep on keeping on. I knew nothing could tear me down at that point because I was through the thick of it and ready to get back to being a normal, functioning human being.

It never really hit me how much schoolwork I had actually missed until the last few weeks at Coelho. My learning disabilities still hindered how quickly I did my work, but I learned to accept them and work through them rather than let them control me. My tutor had run out of assigned work for me to do—I had finally been tenacious about completing assignments. She asked me to contact Mrs. Carter, the English teacher responsible for assigning me work for other assignments. I went to Mrs. Carter's room and introduced myself, and she said, "Wow! It's great to put a face with a name. You were like the mystery student. What can I help you with?"

"I was wondering if there was any other work I missed that I need to do before the end of the year."

She laughed. "You've done about an eighth of the work of everyone else. Anything I give you now would just be busy work. So just focus on your other subjects for now."

I felt a little defeated, but I wasn't surprised. I was just happy to be in school.

God kept me buoyed up as I faced the massive amount of work ahead of me. My family always had a large frame with the famous poem "Footprints in the Sand" displayed in our house, but until my last few weeks at Coelho, I had never actually read it. It deeply resonated with me. In the speaker's saddest and lowest points, the Lord was carrying him. Similarly, when I thought there was no God and would ask Him to prove himself by taking me out of my misery, He was carrying me. God always has a plan for us, and no matter how distant He may seem, He knows each of us by name. I had heard such things in church, but none of it made sense until then. I realized that when I asked God to prove Himself to me, He didn't have to because though I never realized it, He was with me every step of the way.

As the last days of school were wrapping up, I was excited to start the summer and prepare for high school. I knew I would have to continue to do schoolwork throughout the summer to better prepare myself for Bishop Feehan High. I had been accepted despite missing so much school.

As the summer kicked off, I attended the party for the St. Stephan's eighth grade graduation. I was invited because it was held at Lake Pearl in Wrentham, Massachusetts, a restaurant owned by Jarred Lorrusso's family. It was a night full of dancing and entertainment. Once we finished dinner, Sr. Renee said what a great class they were and how sad she was to see them go. Jarred had strategically placed me in the middle of the table, and halfway through her speech, our eyes locked, and I realized she had not seen me yet that night. Taken aback in midsentence, she stopped, walked up to me, and shook my hand. In a shaking voice, she said, "It's nice to see you again." She sat down without finishing her speech. It was obvious to me that when she sent the letter to my father, she thought she would never see me again. Bursting back into her life must have sent her for a loop. I felt that I won in that moment. She could not just send me out with the garbage.

But as the night continued, I felt I didn't belong and had no business being there. I was with all the kids I had known for so long but felt excluded. I asked my dad to take me home early. Mocking stares and strident comments from those I used to trust made me realize that though I hadn't graduated from the school I'd wanted to, I was better off. I was a new person. Everyone in the St. Stephan's class—with the exception of Jarred—thought I was crazy; my former classmates avoided me the entire night.

That summer was the first time in two years I was actually functional. Though I slept for twelve or thirteen hours a day, I had energy to do things. I continued to ride my bike and play hockey every day. I also played all-star baseball for Attleboro. The physical recovery was the hardest thing I have ever endured, but I knew that every bead of sweat that trickled from my pores helped me get a little better.

In August, my family went to Hawaii with another family. On the twelve-hour flight from Newark to Honolulu, I found out I wouldn't attend Bishop Feehan that fall. My dad and I weighed the pros and cons. We came to a mutual agreement that it would be best for me not to attend high school in the fall and instead enter eighth grade for a second time. I had missed so much school, my dad said, and everything I did in high school went toward college. Bishop Feehan had placed me in the lowest level classes because I'd been too sick to take the entrance exam. That made sense to me, but I was upset, though I never showed it. It nearly crushed me knowing that everything I had worked so hard for, all the effort I'd put in, simply hadn't been enough.

My dad's second argument was more convincing to me: I was still sleeping twelve hours a day, and the school day at Bishop Feehan started at 7:40 a.m.—I would have to wake up at 6:15 a.m. No matter how much determination I had, the four antibiotics I was on kept me asleep, and it was while I was sleeping that my body was truly recovering.

I wasn't happy with the decision, but I knew it was what was best for me. My temper problems had gone away, so I could think logically and look at the big picture. My dad reminded me that in the end, it was my decision, but his arguments made sense. There was no way for me to wake up on time consistently, and I'd be so far behind the other kids that it might have killed my growing confidence.

My dad and I discussed my options for schools: St. Stephan's (not likely), St. John's (a local Catholic school), Coelho, Mount St. Charles (a Catholic school in Rhode Island famous for its hockey team), or Saint Mary-Sacred Heart (SMSH) in North Attleboro (the school affiliated with the church my family attended).

I hid my emotions until we arrived at our condo. I locked myself in the first bedroom I saw and bawled my eyes out. I felt defeated because of how hard I'd worked to get to that point in my struggle with Lyme just to have my dad tell me it hadn't been enough. Though that wasn't true, it was the way I felt. For the past few months, the thought of going to high school kept me pushing forward; it represented a start and a finish line. It would end the years of suffering with Lyme, and it would be a time to meet new people and an opportunity to get on with my life. But as I cried, I realized that high school wasn't the end of my Lyme story, and no matter what grade I was in or what school I attended, I still had a lot of work to do.

When we got back home, my dad put a final call in to St. Stephan's. He wanted to see if because we had already paid the tuition for my eighth grade, the funds could carry over to the upcoming school year. It was nothing more than an attempt to save some money. To put it simply, they didn't want me back, and that was fine with me. My dad told me Sr. Renee said I needed a "fresh start." Saint John's started at 8:00 a.m., which didn't work for my recovery. I liked the idea of going back to Coelho, but school there started at 7:30 a.m. Mount St. Charles was a twenty-minute commute and also started at 8:00 a.m. That left SMSH in North Attleboro, which started at 9:00 a.m.

My first inclination was to say that there was no way I was going there. Every Sunday when I went to Mass, I scoffed at the trailer in the parking lot where the seventh and eighth grade classrooms were. I though it to be very strange to go to school in a parking lot. I didn't think I'd be comfortable there. When I said that to my dad, he told me that Father Costa, the priest of Sacred Heart and the chaplain of Bishop Feehan, was making an exception by allowing me to go to SMSH. They had a full class, but he put in a good word for me to be able to attend. That did little to sway my opinion of the place. I didn't want to lower myself by attending SMSH.

For the rest of summer, I was upset about my new predicament. All my hard work seemed like a waste. One of the prouder moments of my battle with Lyme disease was putting "attends Bishop Feehan High School" on my Facebook page once I got my acceptance letter. I was morose and defeated when I learned I'd be attending SMSH for eighth grade instead, and I took the post off my Facebook page.

During that summer, I had many strange thoughts on my mind. I thought about life and why I was here on earth, again questioning my purpose. I wondered why I had fought so hard to get to this point and find out everything wasn't working out the way I wanted it to. As I should have done all along, I turned to prayer. I asked God to be with me throughout my journey.

When these questions arose in my mind, I reminded myself that one of my only wishes in life was to never let anyone suffer physically, mentally, or emotionally the way I did. I recalled the profound impact Dr. Silverblatt had on my life after just one appointment. I aspired to have the ability to change the lives of those around me and to teach others to believe in themselves.

During the two weeks I was in Hawaii without my bike, I started running to clear my mind. My temper turned into a passion to exercise. I was able to express my emotions in a positive way through exercise. Since my joints were feeling up to it, jogging was the next best thing after biking. Running got my heart racing faster, and I got into more of a rhythm that allowed me time to think. I continued running throughout the summer as a way to be by myself and clear my mind of distractions. When I ran, I was alone with my thoughts. I separated myself from the negative thoughts and perceptions others had of me. Running allowed me to realize I was just one being, and I could push myself as far as my legs would take me. I was grateful for the breath cascading into my lungs because it signified living again. I was grateful for the pain in my legs because I finally began to feel again. I was not running away from anything but rather facing my fears and running toward the finish line.

Chapter 15
Unexpected Blessings

In the end, it was my decision. I was so against going to SMSH, and repeating eighth grade that I totally shut myself off from my family again. After I spent the last week of summer in my room, my dad came up with a proposition.

"If you go to SMSH for eighth grade and try the best you can," he said, "I'll give you the difference in tuitions between SMSH and Bishop Feehan." That was an offer I couldn't refuse. I decided that if my dad was willing to pay me $5,000 over the course of the year. $555 a month in cash to go to SMSH, I could try to make the best of it.

As the first day of the new school year approached, I was still very bitter about repeating eighth grade and going to SMSH. Sure, they were being generous, and I was lucky that another student had transferred, so I had a spot, but I didn't care. I felt embarrassed about going back to eighth grade (as if I had really gone in the first place), and I didn't know how I would be received by the kids and what they would think of me or of my past.

A few days before the start of school, I took a tour of SMSH and the modular buildings. The buildings were not as rough as they appeared from the outside, but they were different. The hundred-year-old building and modular buildings in the parking lot showed me just how spoiled I'd been at St. Stephan's, which was about ten times larger than SMSH.

I met with the principal, Mrs. Pexioto, and the eighth-grade teacher, Mrs. Petterson. My story evoked a few tears from the two women, but I was done with crying. They totally understood my situation and said they would be there for me through anything, which was a reassuring statement after over two years of scrutiny and disbelief from so many others. Before the meeting ended, Mrs. Pexioto wiped her tears, put her glasses back on, and said, "You need to promise me one thing."

"What's that?"

"By the end of this year, you need to find one thing you like about this place other than that we start at nine."

We laughed. Similar to the administration at Coelho, I knew after that first meeting that the staff of SMSH would support me during my time of need.

The first day of school came, and I was more nervous than I ever had been to go back to school. It was not just a new year at a new school. I had been socially isolated for over a year and was not sure how "normal" kids would accept me. Sure, I was friendly with the kids at Coelho, but there was a difference between polite passing greetings and a year's worth of conversation with seventeen strangers. I didn't know how they would take it when they found out about my past. *Should I tell them at all? Could I hide it?* In the class of seventeen, fifteen had been together since kindergarten. I have always been a very social person, but I thought it would be arduous if not impossible for me to fit in there.

To help me get better acquainted, I was paired with one of my classmates; Sean Legg showed me the ropes and helped me adjust. My first day was extremely awkward. Everyone was in one or another clique, and I sat off to the side by myself. The class played games and icebreakers all day. It was weird. I was almost frightened by how close my classmates were with each other.

For one activity, we got into groups by the month in which we were born. A few of us were in the January group. From there, Mrs. Petterson arranged us by date in the month. I was the first in my group. "Okay, who's the oldest?" she asked. I bit my lip and gave her a death stare. We locked eyes, and she realized what she had done. "Oh my gosh, I am so sorry," she said. "Guys, Patrick is older." She whispered to me, "Do you want to tell them your story?"

I wanted to cry and storm out of the room, but I composed myself and muttered, "I had Lyme disease and missed all of last year of school." That proved I had better control of my emotions. I knew she didn't mean to put me on the spot, and I forgave her, but that was not the way I had intended to tell my classmates about my past.

The other students were stunned. I was a new student with a story very different from what they were accustomed to. It must have been a lot for them to process. That day, I noticed all the different cliques. No one made an effort to talk to me. The first day finally ended, and I was convinced it would be an awful year that I would spend alone.

My mom had gone to high school with the cross-country coach at SMSH, Mrs. Magill, whose daughter, Carolyn, was in my class. My mom thought joining the team would be a great way for me to make friends and continue running. I wasn't interested in meeting a bunch of twelve-year-olds, but I took it as a free workout. At the first practice, I did meet a few new kids, but I wasn't happy with the situation.

I felt so out of place for the first week of school and cross-country practice. As much as I wanted to be elsewhere, I was stuck there, so I was still desperate to fit in. I got discouraged when that didn't happen right away. One day at cross-country practice, I was running with Brendan Patch, one of the kids from my class. After a few minutes of running together, we started clicking. We had the same sense of humor and interests. Our main connections were based on humor and sports. I mentioned I played baseball, and he seemed overjoyed. He told me the Cubs had drafted his dad as a pitcher years earlier.

As we continued on our run, it seemed as though we had been friends forever. Finally, I had broken through the barrier and began to feel accepted by the class. I started to be more outgoing and social with my classmates.

As we started to get into the curriculum, I gradually realized why I was repeating eighth grade. It was still very difficult for me to focus, read, write, and remember and process information, but compared to the prior year, I was considerably better. I struggled sometimes, but I was once again able to focus. And my writing, though sloppy, was better than it had been. Over the summer, my brain seemed to heal. I had a follow-up scan of the brain lesions that showed that all of them had healed. My reading and writing skills came back as I worked with a neurological recovery therapist.

The first story we read for English was the story of Wilma Rudolph, a track runner who had suffered from polio. We were scheduled to have a test on the story, and I was nervous. I hadn't taken a real test in almost two years. I had no idea how I would do. After studying for a couple hours, rereading the story, and reading online analyses of it, I felt I was prepared. When I took the test, I thought I had done okay but not great. When Mrs. Petterson returned the test a few days later, I hesitantly turned mine over and saw the grade: 76 percent. Although many people might see that as average, I saw it as a huge victory. I had read something and remembered it well enough to perform well on a test, which was the same test the other students had taken. And after the test, I had an accurate sense of how well I'd done even before I'd seen the grade. I was elated. My brain was starting to work the way it had before I contracted Lyme disease.

This huge confidence boost came right before my first cross-country meet that night. I was anxious and nearly jittery. As we drove to Slater Park for the meet, I saw some familiar faces from St. Stephan's, students from the class below me. They welcomed me with open arms and said they were glad I was feeling better. The love I felt from members of that class was reassuring. They hadn't observed the full extent of my symptoms, but they were compassionate.

I found my teammates and started to warm up. I took a warmup lap with Sean.

"You nervous?" he asked.

"Extremely."

"Don't be, man. You'll do great."

"Thanks, but this is my first sports competition in almost a year."

"Just relax. You'll be fine."

I was nervous but confident as the race was about to start. I was the fastest kid on the team in practice, and I was ready to see how I compared to runners from other schools. I inched up to the starting line, breathing heavily with nervousness. I thought the race would never start. When the gun finally went off, I shot off the starting line in a dead sprint. After I got about a fifty-foot lead on the competition, I regretted the sprint as I gasped for air around the first turn. After a half mile, people started to pass me, but I didn't let that stop me. I knew I had put myself into this situation and wasn't going to blame anyone else or be jealous of those overtaking me. I took full responsibility for my life. I was finally realizing that in life, all positions are temporary. I came in thirteenth, running a time of 13:15 for the two-mile course. I was proud of myself for finishing the race and setting a decent benchmark for myself.

We got home at about seven that evening, and I went straight to bed without dinner. I was wiped out physically and mentally. I slept the entire next day and was absent for the first time at SMSH. I woke up at six the following night, still fatigued and with a headache and body aches. When I woke up, I was angry at myself for having missed school. I felt like I was relapsing. In reality, I had just pushed myself too hard. But at the time, I felt it was more than that. I was frightened my symptoms were coming back, that I wasn't better.

My parents and I reconsidered cross-country. That weekend, I recuperated and finished the schoolwork I had missed. For the next two weeks, my parents said they didn't want me to do cross-country but focus instead on my health and schoolwork. I was upset at first because while I was on the team, I had made friends and enjoyed myself for the first time in as long as I could remember.

As the two weeks progressed, I recovered. The rest paid off. Slowly but surely, my test grades went from the seventies to eighties and eventually nineties. After a two-week sabbatical from cross-country, my brain and body felt up to running. I felt even better than I had when I started cross-country. My body was rested, ache-free, and energized. I was engaged and scholarly in the classroom. My parents agreed that it was the right time for me to return to sports.

In my second race of the year, I shaved almost a whole minute off my time. I decided to try out for a hockey team, the Pawtucket Pirates, and I made it. I hadn't played hockey competitively since fourth grade, but I made an elite, AAU hockey team out of all self-teaching and practice. This reinforced the belief that was taking me through my recovery: through hard work and determination, I could accomplish anything I wanted to. I was empowered and invigorated; I had put in the work, and it was paying off.

Through the fall, I continued to succeed at SMSH. I went from having to be paid to go to wanting to go. I finally started to fit in with the other kids and felt accepted. I had a full plate of hockey practices, games, cross-country meets, and homework, but finally, I was physically and mentally up to the challenge. I scored my first hockey goal during our first game at Dennis Lynch Arena in Pawtucket, where I had practiced so many times. I was playing defense, and the puck was passed to me before the blue line. I took a slap shot and watched as it found the back of the net—a euphoric feeling. I felt I could do anything; I was floating. Everything I had dreamed about was coming true. I felt I belonged when my teammates congratulated me. I became human again.

I felt better and better every week. I finally felt like a normal kid again. Every week, I improved on my previous cross-country time and was an impact player on my hockey team. I earned straight A's in school, something I had never done before.

Before I knew it, the cross-country season was ending. Our last meet was the Massachusetts state championship. More than fifty schools and almost 1,000 kids were competing. I was extremely nervous because it was the biggest race I had ever run. Like every other race, I found my teammates. Brendan was especially excited to see me.

He high-fived me. "Are you ready, man?"

"I guess."

"What do you mean?" he asked happily.

"I'm nervous."

"What are you nervous about? You're so much better than these kids."

He put his arm around my shoulders and started to walk with me. He pointed to a group of runners stretching.

"Look," he said. "He has chicken legs, she looks like she's never run before, and that one is only here for the free popsicles after the race. He doesn't even know where the starting line is."

I couldn't control my laughter. Brendan always had an uncanny ability to make me laugh. "I guess you're right."

"Hey." He shook my hand. "We're finishing this thing together, okay?"

I was motivated. "Let's do it."

Brendan and I took our warm-up lap and realized how many runners were there; we couldn't find a spot to warm up. As the mob lined up at the starting line, I felt squished by the others. Brendan was next to me. He looked me in the eyes before the start as if to say, *It's gonna be okay.*

We all took off at the sound of the gun. Brendan and I stayed together the whole way. We worked as a team, staying shoulder to shoulder on the narrow path to make sure no one could pass. The faster kids behind us pushed us beyond our normal limits.

After the first mile, my legs began to cramp. My body was telling me I couldn't push it that hard. Agonizing pain took over my entire body, and I thought back to why I had started working out. I was trying to save my life. I had started biking because everyone else had given up on me, and I was the only one who believed in myself—and even I had my doubts.

As we got closer to the end, Brendan and I realized we were in the front of the pack with the top twenty-five runners. I told him we should push it on the last quarter mile, and he agreed. We passed five or six more people, and in the process, I passed Brendan. I have no regrets about leaving him behind. I wouldn't have been pushed to run as well as I had without him.

I made the final turn. I could see the finish line. I saw the clock ticking upward one second at a time. I saw my coach at the finish line cheering me on. There were hundreds of people along the sides cheering. The end still felt far away. I was tired. But the pain I felt was small compared to the pain of the last three years of my life. During those years, the pain had kept me in bed. The fatigue had kept me asleep. The whole experience had kept me in a state of frustration and debilitating anger. As I ran, I remembered all the evil that one little tick had created. And it pushed me forward.

I was running faster and faster as hard as I could go. I glanced at the clock; I knew I was going to shatter my 12:15 record. I pulled energy from nowhere and surged toward the finish. I passed the line in tenth place. The only source of my energy was pure determination.

Exhausted yet exhilarated, I pounded my chest twice and pointed to the sky to God. I had tried to leave God when I was sick, but He had never left me. I felt chills throughout my entire body, a free and joyful feeling. I couldn't hear anything for about ten seconds; it was during that meditative period with God that I realized He had done all this for a reason—to make me a stronger and better person than I ever was before, than I ever could've been without this struggle.

Through my recovery, I found the kind of person I want to be, but most important, I found God. The doctors had misdiagnosed me. I was sick for years. I had to repeat eighth grade. But God never left me— not even when I turned away. Since my near-death experience, I have realized that God has very important plans for me to serve Him as best I could. I was intended to help those who cannot help themselves and those who have lost all hope. I was intended to have a profound impact on everyone I meet because of what I learned about life through my story of resiliency.

After I came back to reality, Mrs. Magill told me I had broken my personal record and the school's cross-country record, something that had not been done in five years. That proved that through God all things are possible. That moment made it all worth it. All the struggle I had gone through pushing myself to exercise, all the miles I ran and biked during my recovery from Lyme and in my preparation for this race. The agony I experienced, the suicidal thoughts and actions that hindered me so greatly, all the times I'd wanted to quit but instead pushed forward. They were all worth it because I finally had a purpose. It finally made sense.

Chapter 16
My New Life

The following day, I was greeted by a myriad of staff and students who congratulated me on my feat. Seemingly, everyone in the school knew about my record-breaking performance (and everyone did know about it when it was announced over the intercom at the end of the school day). Students and teachers I had never met before went out of their way to tell me what a great job I had done. When I saw Brendan, he hugged me and said, "I'm really proud of you man." I had seldom experienced that feeling of belonging during my Lyme journey.

My friendship with Brendan turned out to be very significant. Crossing the finish line of the race marked my conquering Lyme disease and the beginning of the rest of my life. I applied my newfound optimism to interacting with teachers and students. I started making the most of everything and live life to the fullest, the way I had always done before my illness.

The cross-country season was over; I started lifting weights to gain some muscle for the hockey season and with the hopes of playing football in high school—it also helped when I picked up basketball and track later in the year. Using the money my parents paid me to go to SMSH—thinking about that feels strange now—I got a personal trainer at the YMCA. Weight training is analogous to life: the more you put into it, the more you get out of it. It also reminded me of what I had heard before: "You're going to get worse before you get better." While lifting, you go through so much pain and agony to progress. But I had been through worse pain before—emotionally, physically, mentally, and spiritually.

In order to become the strongest version of myself, I needed to let go of any lingering attachment to St. Stephan's. If I continued to think about what I could have been, I'd miss who I was and who I wanted to become. One of the many things I was resentful about after leaving St. Stephan's was not being able to do the eighth grade art project. All the eighth graders had designed and created their own chairs to sit in at graduation. I had started mine during my short time there in eighth grade; I had planned on reupholstering an old rolling chair. After I was asked to leave St. Stephan's, the administration removed all my belongings from my locker, including my laptop, and threw them out without even notifying me or my parents. They wanted to throw out the chair, but the art teacher wouldn't let them.

Mrs. Sweet, the art teacher at SMSH, asked me what we did in art class in eighth grade at St. Stephan's. After I told her about the chairs, she wanted to have us do the same project. After a little bit of convincing, the principal, Mrs. Pexioto, approved it. All the kids went to yard sales and thrift stores in search of the perfect chair.

I found mine at Savers, a thrift store. I had my whole chair already planned out in my head. I was going to upholster a chair and turn it into a giant hockey skate. After countless hours of working on the chair, it was perfect—exactly the way I had envisioned it. I added laces and a "blade," which made it look much more convincing.

A year of bonding with my classmates and dominating in almost every sport was coming to an end, and graduation rapidly approached. I was somewhat nervous about my impending departure from the school I had grown to love. At the beginning of the year, Mrs. Pexioto made me promise that over the course of the year I would find one thing I liked about SMSH, besides the fact that classes started later than at other schools. At the end of the year, I wrote her a letter listing all the reasons I stayed—and why I loved every moment I was there.

The final day of school finished with a prayer and a parade around the school. It was a very emotional experience for me. As I walked out the door for the last time, I hugged my teachers and Mrs. Pexioto, thanking them for everything they had done for me. Appreciation is not a strong enough word to express the gratitude I felt for them. The administration had taken me in when no one else would, embodying the Beatitudes, which St. Stephan's preached but neglected to practice. I had found holy people who practiced what they preached. This restored my trust in others and my faith in humanity.

That night during our graduation Mass, I felt I was with family. As he was giving the homily, Father Dave said, "This class has a very special bond. Whether they have been here since kindergarten or for only one year, each student in this class is a part of the Saint Mary-Sacred Heart family." As he said that, he winked at me. I felt accepted. Father Costa had made all this happen.

When it was time to accept our diplomas, I was nervous. My palms were sweaty as I pondered the last two years of my life. As I waited to accept my diploma, I remembered all the great things I had done that year, my second year of eighth grade. I thought about the worst and best two years of my life. I thought about all the struggle and doubts I had experienced. I thought about the wonderful things I had accomplished and the friends I had made.

The parents and families sitting in the congregation were instructed at the beginning of Mass to hold their applause until the end of the graduation as to not give any one student special recognition. However, I was an exception. The majority of the parents attending the Mass were aware of the struggle I had been through to get there and walk across that stage. As my name was called, the crowd burst into applause. No one cheered louder than my own family, though.

After I accepted my diploma and hugs from Fr. Dave and Mrs. Pexioto, the ovation continued. Tears streamed down my face as the entire congregation stood in acknowledgment of my resiliency. I was overcome with the feeling that I had finally been accepted. I experienced the presence of God in the church. I had a feeling that this had been a part of His plan all along. I waved in thanks and took my seat after hugging several of my classmates. I no longer felt alone in my battle.

I thought about the "Footprints" prayer, and I realized that all these everyday angels had been carrying me. I realized I was not alone then, nor was I ever alone in my journey. I no longer dwell on my current situation, as I know that it is bound to change. I gained faith in God's plan for me. Life is temporary, and so is pain; the trick is to never quit. Lance Armstrong once said, "Pain is temporary. It may last for a minute, an hour, or a day, or a year, but, eventually, it will subside and something else will take its place. If I quit, however, it lasts forever." This was so true for my life during my lowest times. If I quit, if I gave up, if I accepted my prognosis as terminal, I never would have experienced the life I live now.

I now live a life in which I trust that my current situation isn't permanent. That gives me the power, the ability, and the courage to push through my struggles and become who I want to be. This also keeps me humble in prosperous times because I consider the depths to which I had sunk.

God never intends suffering to happen; He carried me the whole way. My journey taught me to have faith. Though every point in my life seemed arbitrary at the time, I now realize that each twist and turn along the way has made me the man I am today. After winning my battle with Lyme disease, I now understand the meaning of faith. Faith means believing the path is there and taking the next step even when I cannot clearly see the path in front of me. This belief has allowed me to live my life more purposefully, to shoot for my goals, and to believe I create my destiny.

The doctors tried to write my story, but I—and God—had a bigger plan. This chapter in my life is finished, but my story is far from over. I have learned to take responsibility for my life and control only what I can control. I realize I am the only one who has the ability to change my life. I am the author of my own story, and my last chapter hasn't been written yet.

Epilogue
Lyme Is Real; So Is God

When you get into a tight place and everything goes against you, till it seems as though you could not hold on a minute longer, never give up then, for that is just the place and time that the tide will turn.
—Harriet Beecher Stowe

I could have believed the doctors; I could have rolled over and lived my life the way they said I would. I could have been useless to the world and totally dependent on my parents, or I could have been a patient in a mental institution. I could have been tutored for an hour a day until I was eighteen and then lived with my parents for the rest of my life. But what I could or should have been is not who I am now. I am the author of my own story. I dictate my own fate and block out those who don't believe in me. Because of my battle with Lyme disease, I now have the faith and the resiliency to overcome any obstacle and achieve my dreams. I now know God will always be with me because He would never abandon one of His children, someone He loves.

God has a plan for us all. No matter how big or small, it does exist; it's always there. Every time I tell my story, I'm asked, "Why do bad things happen to good people?" The simple answer is that bad things do not exist nor do good things; good and bad are nothing more than perception. For instance, finishing a cross-country meet may just be finishing for some people, but for me, it was the beginning of the rest of my life, the pinnacle of my journey, my transcendence from a life with Lyme disease to one beyond.

During my thirteen sheltered years, I hadn't experienced struggle.

I lived in the safety zone created for me. I had all I had ever desired: I built an electric car, I was a local celebrity, I was a respectable athlete, and I had countless friends. One little tick changed the course of my life more than anything I had ever experienced.

My experience is a testament to the significance of everything that happens in life. It made me question who I was and what life was as I searched for a light in my world of darkness. It made me fall into an endless pit of self-loathing and despair. Not until I attempted suicide did I realize God had been carrying me through all the hard times just as in the "Footprints" prayer. In my time of need, I cursed God for giving me Lyme disease, but now, I praise Him for it. I am thankful for my struggles because they inspired my triumphs. It is because of the struggles I went through spiritually and physically that I am devoted to God and as strong physically and morally as I am now. I am thankful for every second of my life because I know what it's like to be on the brink of death.

Lyme disease is often misunderstood, and the medical community doesn't know what to do about it. Of the hundreds of tests the doctors ran, only one came back positive.[7] Lyme disease is recognized as an acute illness, but chronic Lyme disease is not. Until the results of my SPECT scan came back, which revealed the seven lesions in my brain, there was no evidence to support my suffering. Lacking evidence of a physical malady, countless medical professionals considered me mentally ill.

I am living proof that chronic Lyme is real. According to the Centers for Disease Control, Lyme disease is the fastest growing vector-borne infectious disease in the United States,[8] but most cases are concentrated in the Northeast and Upper Midwest.[9] The CDC estimates that 61 percent of confirmed Lyme cases in 2014 came from just four states: Pennsylvania, Massachusetts, New York, and New Jersey.[10] About 329,000 Americans are diagnosed with Lyme disease each year, making it the largest disease outbreak since AIDS in the 1990s.[11] By no means am I belittling other diseases—my mother fought cancer for nearly four years—but Lyme needs the same level of attention and significance. Unfortunately, "Lyme research only receives $25 million a year in funding, while many of the other infectious diseases receive between

$100 and $200 million annually. HIV now receives over $3 billion a year."[12]

Today, Lyme disease is hardly recognized. If not for my family ties in the Lyme community, I would have been lost in my search for a cure. According to the National Institute of Health,[13] of the estimated 329,000 new cases of Lyme, only $133 is spent per patient. This is in comparison to the funding per patient for HIV/AIDS, which is $57,960. Also, $7,050 is spent per patient with West Nile virus, though there are only 5,700 cases each year.

The real issue at hand is that health insurance companies do not cover long-term antibiotics for the treatment of chronic Lyme disease.[14] In November 2015, the International Lyme and Associated Diseases Society issued Lyme treatment guidelines based on the latest scientific evidence,[15] but many insurance companies won't pay for the treatments at this time. Because Lyme doesn't kill as many people as do other diseases, it is not seen as serious. The instruction in my suicide note was, "Put Lyme disease as my cause of death. Then maybe someone will care."

I am also a living testament that long-term and intravenous antibiotics do work. Over the course of forty-five days, I went from being nearly in a coma, having seizures almost every day, being unable to read or write, and not being able to function to being the lively, energetic, personable kid I was pre-Lyme. Through much dedication and hundreds of hours working with a neurological ophthalmologist, by the time I finally made it to high school, my reading and writing abilities were back to full capacity. Though my handwriting is clumsy and my reading is a bit slow, I am now performing well above grade level in all academic fields. The antibiotics that cured my illness and my divine motivation to get better drove me to a full recovery.

Lyme disease is real. The symptoms crushed my quality of life so much that I attempted to end my life. If not for God, who knows where I would be right now in my life, or in my Lyme—and faith—journey. My faith led me out of my suffering as God showed me the light. Fate allowed me to go to SMSH and be surrounded by the people of God. Resiliency kept me from giving up and allowing the doctors' words to stop me. Instead, I set three athletic school records at SMSH just a year after I was sleeping twenty-three hours a day and could barely walk.

I overcame Lyme disease, and I am the man I am now because of it. Though this is the end of my journey with Lyme disease, my life is just beginning. The road of life is uncharted and ambiguous, but no matter what comes my way, I now know that Helen Keller was correct when she said, "A bend in the road is not the end unless you fail to make the turn." If people ever tell you that you cannot do something, they're wrong—look all your doubters square in the eye and say, "Watch me!" When you find God and the mission He has for you, no one can stop you. Resiliency is not an esoteric quality possessed only by the great among us, but rather, it is inside us all waiting for us to find our true purposes in life. When you're suffering, know that God is there. He will help you through if you work hard and listen to Him.

Notes

1 http://www.webmd.com/add-adhd/childhood-adhd/news/20110418/study-adhd-linked-preterm-birth#.

2 http://thericatholic.com/stories/St. Stephan-scientists-convert-car-to-electric-power,2845?

3 http://www.massgeneral.org/conditions/condition.aspx?id=281&display=treatments.

4 https://www.lymedisease.org/lyme-basics/co-infections/about-co-infections/.

5 https://chronicillnessrecovery.org/index.php?option=com_content&view=article&id=161.

6 http://www.lymediseaseaction.org.uk/about-lyme/neurology-psychiatry/.

7 https://www.bostonglobe.com/lifestyle/health-wellness/2013/10/20/many-tests-diagnose-lyme-but-proof-they/ISjAcxmZxkk2disi94ENfI/story.html.

8 http://www.bayarealyme.org/about/.

9 http://www.cdc.gov/Lyme/Stats/Index.html.

10 http://www.cdc.gov/Lyme/Stats/Tables.html.

11 http://www.truth-out.org/news/item/21206-from-AIDS-to-Lyme-will-we-let-history-repeat-itself.

12 Ibid.

13 http://www.nih.gov.

14 http://www.insurancequotes.com/health/lyme-disease-health-insurance.

15 www.ilads.org/ilads_news/2015/ilads-treatment-guidelines-are-now-summarized-on-the-national-guideline-clearinghouse-website-/.

About the Author

Patrick Collins is a passionate, driven, curious, and generous young man from Attleboro, Massachusetts. His unique perspective, gained during his arduous battle with Lyme disease, and story of resiliency will be truly inspiring and empowering to all of his readers.

Made in the USA
Middletown, DE
30 July 2017